D0473042

TAKE IT HOME

Inspiration and Events to Help Parents Spiritually Transform Their Children

- Connects kids with Christ beyond their church and into the home
- Equips children's pastors to become a resource to parents in the congregation
- Promotes spiritual formation for all ages
- Includes a special "parent equipping" event for each age level
- Suggests resources for families to use at home
- **REPRODUCIBLE!**

CD-ROM INCLUDED

MARK HOLMEN AND DAVE TEIXEIRA

Guidelines for Photocopying Reproducible Pages

Editorial Staff

Senior Managing Editor, Sheryl Haystead • **Contributing Editor,** Jean Lawson • **Editorial Assistant,** Ellen Lewellyn • **Art Director,** Lenndy Pollard, • **Designer,** Annette M. Chavez

Founder, Dr. Henrietta Mears • **Publisher,** William T. Greig • **Senior Consulting Publisher,** Dr. Elmer L. Towns • **Senior Consulting Editor,** Wesley Haystead, M.S.Ed.

Contents

Introduction

Included in this guidebook are outlines for 13 Take It Home Events for infants through high school students and their parents. The purpose of each Take It Home Event is to "teach a family how to fish" rather than simply providing them a meal of fish. If we want to reestablish the home as the primary place where spiritual growth is nurtured, we must get back to the basics of training parents in the essential faith skills that must take place in the home.

Please note that this guidebook does not provide an exhaustive list of events as there are many more Take It Home Events that churches are doing all over the world. That is why we have developed a website for churches to share Take It Home Event ideas and resources. That website is www.faithbeginsathome.com.

I encourage you to take a look at the event outlines in this guidebook with the idea of customizing them to your situation. I have implemented Take It Home Events in four different congregations and they have never been the same. In one church we may have taught parents how to pray with their kids at four years old and at another church we did it with third graders and in each situation the event was done in a different way. The key is to implement the strategy of Take It Home Events into your ministry to children and youth in a way that works in your setting. The outlines in this guidebook will help you think through the process and develop a strategy. May the Lord bless you as you develop this ministry that will help bring Christ into the center of every family in your congregation.

In Take It Home Events, you will support families and empower Mom and Dad to be effective in training and teaching their children about Christ in three ways: equip them, encourage them, and help create shared faith experiences for them. The Take It Home Events provided in this guidebook focus on specific aspects of discipleship.

Baby Dedication or Infant Baptism: For Families with Newborns

Some churches dedicate young children to the Lord. Others baptize infants. Whatever service your church has to acknowledge the value and priority of raising children in the ways of God must be more than simply a ritual. If it were nothing more than a ritual, it would have little, if any, lasting impact. Yet, as we seize the opportunity to be intentional in dedicating children, this act can become a powerful first step in establishing the parents as the most important faith influencers. The home is the primary place where faith is nurtured and the church becomes a lifelong partner in equipping parents to pass on the faith to their child. This Take It Home Event will provide ideas for how you can approach that meeting or class as well as the dedication or baptism itself.

Family Blessings: For Families with Two-Year-Olds

If begun early, the habit of praying God's blessings over children will open the door for God's blessing and for intimate faith talk between parents and children that will bear fruit in years to come. This event will provide many Scriptural blessings a family can use.

Family Devotions: For Families with Three-Year-Olds

The most precious commodity in our world today is time. We don't have enough of it. And this problem is perhaps most evident in the lives of families where the schedules of multiple persons converge in one home. Families have a hard time even sitting down at the table for dinner let alone carving out time for God together. It is no wonder that George Barna reports that fewer than 10 percent of parents who regularly attend church have consistent family time with God.[1] It wasn't a part of their routine at home as a child and so it has not become a practice in their lives today. At some point we must help our families break this cycle. This Take It Home Event will help families establish the habit of having family devotions.

My Church: For Families with Preschoolers or Four-Year-Olds

What is the church? Is it just a place we go every Sunday or is it something more? How do I fit in at my church and why is it so important? In this Take It Home Event you will answer some of these questions about the church and more importantly help kids and families experience and understand what a very important part of the faith community they are. They will understand that the church is not just a building, but also an extended family. You will help families to be familiar with and feel comfortable in the building where their church meets.

While most of the Take It Home Events focus on equipping and encouraging parents to implement faith in the home, this event is a little different. It is more focused on the experience of empowering families to live for Christ.

Family Prayer: For Families with Kindergartners or Five-Year-Olds

At the very heart of the Christian life lies communication with God through prayer. In fact, Martin Luther King, Jr. once said, "To be a Christian without prayer is no more possible than to be alive without breathing."[2] Unfortunately, many Christians don't regularly engage God through prayer because it was not built into their lives as children. While many adults must make a concerted effort to spend regular time in prayer, our goal for the next generation is that prayer will become a regular habit, a reflex reaction, something they naturally and instinctively engage in because from a very young age it became a part of who they are.

As you train parents to pray with their children, you are basically teaching them to pray on the most basic level. Ultimately, it is Prayer Class 101. The great thing about this from my experience is that when it comes to prayer, many parents are in the same place as these kids. They have very little personal experience with regular, consistent prayer. So, as you teach them to pray with their children, you are simultaneously training parents how they can pray personally. It's beautiful, because what might come off as childish, silly, embarrassing or condescending when being taught to a group of adults alone, can be effective coming from the angle of teaching to pray with their kids.

Family Service Projects: For Families with First Graders

With our children growing up in a "what's in it for me?" society, how can we help them care about and be willing to serve others in response to God's love for them? This Take It Home Event will motivate families to go beyond simply hearing and talking about ways to love and obey God.

Family Worship: For Families with Second Graders

Most families don't worship at home because no one has equipped them to do so ("I don't know how to plan a worship. I'll probably do it wrong.") This is a common fear most people have when it comes to planning and leading a worship service. These fears are not necessary because planning and leading worship in your home is easy, meaningful and fun. This Take It Home Event will teach parents what worship is and how to do it with their family.

My Bible: For Families with Third Graders

How many people in our world today wish they knew more about the Bible? How many Christians wish they had the discipline to spend more time reading God's Word? How many times have Christians been in situations where they wish they could reference the authority and power of Scripture but have been unable to recall the passage or verse they are thinking of. What if the Bible became a part of who we are as people? What if from a very early age the stories, history and truth of God's Story became a part of our story? What if people, when they talked about Scripture, didn't just refer to a book that sat on the shelf and collected dust, but were connected to that book in such a way that it shaped the very core of who they were? What if it wasn't just "the Bible" but truly became "my Bible"? This Take It Home Event will make this a reality for families in your church.

Money and Me: For Families with Fourth and Fifth Graders

Habits are formed at home and very early in life. And more and more kids are encountering, dealing with and developing their money-handling habits earlier and earlier. In addition, very few parents give their kids any training on how to handle money effectively. As a result, for many people in our society, money is not being controlled by them, but controlling them. Combine this with the fact that Jesus frequently addressed the subject of money and we may safely assume that how we learn to deal with money will be a significant factor in our spiritual growth and development. Families can learn together how to handle their finances in this Take It Home Event.

Computer Safety: For Families with Teenagers

We often refer to the world of computers and the Internet as the "cyber" or "virtual" world. When we do, we sometimes get the impression that what happens on the computer isn't real or somehow doesn't count. This is far from true! For many teens today, the cyber world is where they really live. They shop, talk, study, entertain, socialize and do numerous other activities sitting comfortably at home in front of a computer

screen. But just like the physical world, the cyber world can be dangerous and parents need to set boundaries and enforce rules to protect their children from harm and danger. This can be difficult to do when parents are unfamiliar with how life on the web works, where the dangers lie and how to implement and monitor rules. When I was a kid, there was a classic commercial on television encouraging parents to be active in protecting their kids. The punch line to this ad asked, "It's 10 p.m. Do you know where your children are?" If it were only that simple today! Sitting safely in their own room kids can literally be making plans with friends, talking with strangers, purchasing forbidden items, or viewing explicit materials. "It is 3:00 in the afternoon, do you really know where your children are?"

As a response to this reality, parents often act in one of two opposite ways. They either decide that computers, the Internet and cyberspace are evil and ban their children from ever visiting this forbidden land, or they throw up their hands and let their kids roam the virtual world with no supervision or restrictions. At this Take It Home Event we want to help parents find a balanced approach. Fear and avoidance are responses that stem from not having enough information and experience.

Faith Mentoring—Establishing Another Voice: For Families with Teenagers

As teenagers begin the journey into high school, they naturally begin to seek out the perspective and "voices" of other people. Teenagers need other adults in addition to their parents, teachers and pastors with whom they can talk about faith and life issues. In a Search Institute report only 41 percent of youth felt that adults in the church cared for them.[3] This event will help your teens and your church strengthen relationships between generations that will spiritually guide your children as they continue to develop. It includes an orientation session, a six-week mentoring program and a wrap-up session.

Talking About Dating, Kissing, Sex and Stuff: For Families with Teenagers

The issues of dating, sex and relationships are some of the biggest questions, challenges, and struggles teens face. Messages, temptations, information and even opportunities are regularly offered by society when it comes to sexual experiences, and yet, the Church has been reluctant to engage teens in authentic conversations. Likewise, parents who are often intimidated, overwhelmed and disengaged from their kids' sexual struggles have received little or no support from the Church on how to instruct and guide their children towards healthy sexual development and activity. How can the body of Christ help students work through their struggles, challenging them to dis-

cover how God might guide and direct their sexual choices? Furthermore, how might the Church empower parents to engage in open, honest and value-passing conversations with their teens, providing much needed support for them as they seek to live in a radically counter-cultural way? This Take It Home Event will be a starting place in creating an event that is right for your families.

Looking into the Future—Spiritual Gifts: For Families with Teenagers

Some teens seem to know just what it is they want to do with their lives, while others are overwhelmed by the choices and decisions they are facing. This Take It Home Event will provide the reassurance that God gives gifts to each person to accomplish amazing things—no matter what his or her daily job might be.

Notes

1. George Barna, *Transforming Children into Spiritual Champions* (Ventura, CA: Regal Books, 2003), p. 78.

2. www.brainyquote.com (accessed September 2007).

3. Peter Benson, *What Kids Need to Succeed* (Minneapolis, MN: Spirit Publishers, 1998), p. 36.

Section I

Becoming a Church *of* Family Ministry

Why Family Ministry?

Not long ago, my wife, Maria, was reading a magazine article as she ran on the treadmill. The article was about how to add 30 minutes to your day. The last suggestion almost made her fall off the treadmill. One woman proudly stated that she'd found a way to get two hours more out of her week by dropping her kids off at church and running errands while they were in Sunday School. The article pointed out a startling reality that for many families today, the church is no more than a safe drop-off center for kids. I don't think this was God's intention when He created the Church.

I agree with researcher George Barna when he writes, "The local church should be an intimate and valuable partner in the effort to raise the coming generation of Christ's followers and church leaders, but it is the parents whom God will hold primarily accountable for the spiritual maturation of their children."[1] The key word for me in his statement is "partner." While I wholeheartedly believe that the local church can be the MVP—Most Valuable Partner—for families, I'm convinced that the church also needs a makeover.

The Church Makeover

One reason the local church is no longer seen as a valuable partner for families isn't really a problem with the church at all. It's the reality that families no longer seem to have time for church. Just a few decades ago, the church played a much more significant role in the lives of families. It wasn't unusual to see businesses closed on Sundays, and public schools wouldn't give homework on Wednesdays because it was church night. Families were committed to being at church whenever the doors were open.

Today, however, hardly anyone even recognizes the concept of "church night." Sunday morning is business as usual. If anything, the church now competes with sports leagues and many other extracurricular activities that vie for the family's time—even on Sunday mornings. I believe that Satan knows that the Christian Church is one of the most valuable resources families need in order to succeed, so he'll do everything he can to keep people from getting connected to an intentional Christian community. One of the tools he uses is to keep families so busy that they don't have time for church. And quite simply, when you don't have time for church, you can't establish a lasting partnership with the church.

Another reason the church is not seen as a valuable partner is that many families don't recognize the local church as a resource to help them with family relationships. People will turn to TV and radio shrinks, the Internet, counseling and even

medication to help their family. But the church isn't even a blip on their radar.

I once worked with a family that had been through an ugly divorce. The parents battled almost every situation through lawsuits and court cases. They tried counseling but quit out of frustration. As is often the case, the children found themselves continually in the middle of their parents' warfare. I became involved in the situation because the teenaged daughter in the family, Abby, started attending our youth worship service at the invitation of a school friend. Eventually, Abby joined a small group and began to open up. Things came to a head one Friday night when she came to church and asked to meet with me. She informed me that her mom was home drunk because she'd just had another fight with her ex-husband. Abby didn't know what to do. We called her mom and got permission for her to stay at her friend's house that evening. The next day, I went over to meet with Abby's mom. When I arrived, I was greeted rather abruptly with, "Who are you and what do you want?"

"My name is Pastor Mark," I said as politely as I could. "Abby is part of our youth group, and I was wondering if we could talk for a minute."

Somewhat surprised and a bit ashamed, Abby's mother responded more softly, "I'm sorry, I thought you were a door-to-door salesman." She invited me in, and after a few minutes I informed her that Abby had told me about the divorce and the drinking problem. I asked if there was anything I could do to help. The look of brokenness in her eyes said it all, and she struggled to reply.

I looked her in the eyes and said softly, "Ma'am, I'm not here to judge you or to preach to you. I just want you to know that you, your children and even your ex-husband matter to God. And we'd welcome the opportunity to show you how Christ wants to help you and your family."

Abby's mom broke into tears. After a few moments, she replied, "I used to go to church before all this happened. But after all of this mess, I thought the church was only for families who had it all together and that I no longer was welcome or belonged."

Over the course of the next two years, our church was able to come alongside this family and see God work many miracles. Abby now attends a Christian college and is studying to become a youth pastor. Her mom has made a complete turnaround and is now remarried to a wonderful Christian man.

While Abby's story is great news, the point I'm trying to make is that the church needs to get back on the radar for families. If it hadn't been for Abby, her mom probably would never have set foot in her local church during her time of crisis and need. Whether she was right or wrong, she had the church pegged as a place only for families that are healthy and "have it together." The Church as a whole needs to break this stereotype and put out a welcome mat that reads, "All families are welcome here."

Jesus as the Center

I once read a *USA Today* article that described the different forms of family that exist in our culture today. For example, a single mother is one form of family. A dual income, no kids (DINK) couple is another form of family. Do you know how many forms of family this article identified? Twenty-eight! While we could argue the strengths and weaknesses of each form of family, I can tell you with certainty that each form of family needs the same thing to succeed: Jesus Christ in the center of family life.

Where are you going to learn about that and see it in action? From the media? In public schools? Unfortunately not, which is why you need the local church. George Barna writes, "It is true, though, that a family can benefit from the help of a supportive community [the church], especially when that community is grounded in the Christian faith—a faith that is genuine, unchanging, readily accessible, focused on what matters to God and based on love and truth."[2]

When I lead a new-member class at our church, I stress the importance of the church as a partner to families. I begin by saying, "If you're looking for a place where you can drop off your children and expect us to teach them the faith, then you need to look for another church, because we're not the right church for you." I continue by explaining that our church believes the home is the primary place where faith is nurtured and that parents are to be the primary nurturers. While we believe this unwaveringly, our church also recognizes that the majority of families today probably have no idea how to make their home a place for nurturing the faith of their children. So we desire to come alongside them, as a lifelong partner, and equip them to bring the love of Jesus Christ into the center of their homes and family life. We believe that only this will lead to families being healthy and whole.

"If you need to know how to pray in the home, we'll teach you," I explain to the new-member class. "If you need to know how to do family devotions in the home, we'll show you. If you need help talking to your teenager about sex, we'll come alongside you with resources to help you. And if you need an elderly couple to serve as mentors or adopted grandparents for your children, we'll help you find them." To me, this is the role of the church—to be a valuable and necessary partner to families.

Deena and her husband were the parents of two beautiful children, one age nine and the other just a few months old. Deena had been moved by one of my messages regarding the role that parents play in passing on faith to their children. As a result, she made a personal commitment to bring Christ into the center of her life and the life of her family. She called and set up a time to have their youngest child dedicated.

One week before the dedication, Deena called to tell me that her child had died of SIDS. The loss was devas-

tating. I realized how difficult this would be for Deena, so I began to pray for her. Two months later, Deena came to a baptism class that I was leading. When it came time for her to share her personal testimony, Deena tearfully, yet calmly, shared about the loss of her baby and how devastating it had been for her. She went on to tell how much more important God had become to her as a result. She said the church had carried her through the difficult days. She was overwhelmed by the love that the people in the church had showered upon her and her family. She was thankful that she'd gotten to know about God's love for her before this tragedy happened. She knew that God was the source of strength and peace she was experiencing. Now she wanted to be baptized to publicly show that in spite of her pain and unanswered questions, God would continue to be at the center of her life and the life of her family.

On the Sunday Deena was baptized, there wasn't a dry eye in the place. Now, two years later, God has blessed Deena and her husband with another child. Deena has repeatedly said, "I really don't know what I would have done without God and this church. We didn't even know most of these people personally, but they carried us through. They showered us with the love of Christ when we needed it most."

I firmly believe that Christ, through the church, has something to offer you and your family that you can't find anywhere else. The loving arms of Jesus Christ were able to wrap themselves around Deena and her family in their time of need because they had a relationship with the Bride of Christ, the Church. The truth is that all families will face times when they could use the loving arms of Christ to carry them through their pain or need. That's why Christ gave us the Church—a fellowship of believers who aren't perfect. But through Christ, they become the perfect comforters in our time of crisis.

A Family Ministry Vision

Recent statistics from Search Institute reveal that mom and dad are the top influencers in the faith development of children, yet further data depicts a more alarming reality. While mom and dad are the top influencers in the faith development of children, only 12 percent of churched youth have ever talked with their mom about faith, only 5 percent of churched youth have talked with their dad about faith and only 9 percent of churched youth have experienced either family devotions, prayer or Bible reading in the home. And these statistics are from churched families.[3]

Therefore, while parents are the primary influencers in passing on faith, the majority are not actively engaged in passing on faith themselves. If we want our children to have a faith that is "impressed on their hearts," as Deuteronomy 6 depicts, the church must get back to training and equip-

ping parents to talk about the commands to love and obey God "wherever you are, sitting at home or walking in the street; talk about them from the time you get up in the morning to when you fall into bed at night." (Deuteronomy 6:7, *THE MESSAGE*).

Take a look at what some others are saying about the need for family ministry today.

"If you're not doing family ministry, you're not doing youth ministry." —Tom Schultz, Group Publishing[4]

"The church's role is to be equippers of families. What we ought to do is let the kids drop their parents off at church, train the parents and send them back to their mission field, their home, to grow Christians." —Dr. Roland Martinson, noted at a Youth and Family Institute conference[5]

I believe one of the greatest existing challenges facing the North American church today is trying to figure out *how* we can equip the home to be the primary place where faith is nurtured *through* our existing ministry structures.

This *Take It Home* implementation guide has been designed to give your church a beginning framework for a family ministry that can be woven into your existing ministry with children and youth that will equip the home to once again be the primary place where faith is nurtured. This model is designed to get you started and pointed in the right direction, yet leaves plenty of room for you to customize it to your specific ministry context.

Please hear what I am not saying: I do not believe we need to throw the baby out with the bathwater and eliminate or completely change Sunday School, vacation Bible school, youth ministry, camps, retreats, etc. I have experienced how effective these programs are in passing on faith to children and youth. Yet I do believe we need to take a serious look through the lens of equipping mom and dad at how we are doing these ministries. Why? No matter how effective these ministries are, mom and dad are two to three times more influential than any church program. Therefore shouldn't we devote some considerable time, effort and resources to what is most effective and God ordained?

Please hear what I am saying: I love the Church and I believe God is calling the Church to rise up and address the area that Satan is attacking the most: our families. My experience over the past 12 years has shown me that parents today want to have a better family than the one they grew up in, and they are searching for a better way to "do family." I firmly believe the Christian church has what every family needs to succeed. A personal, growing relationship with Jesus Christ who is standing at the door of their home knocking, saying, "Let me in and I will help your family enjoy long life!" Now is the time for the church to come alongside families and equip them to bring Christ into the center of their homes. As a pastor I served with once said to me, "The role of the church is not to make sure that as you look down on this community you can see the light shining bright from our campus/facility. The role of the church is to make sure the light is shining in each and every home so the community can be lit for the world to see!"

A Family Ministry Model

Over the past 15 years, as churches have become more aware of the need for a strong family ministry, I have witnessed the emergence of two family ministry models. The first model is what I affectionately call the "Add-a-

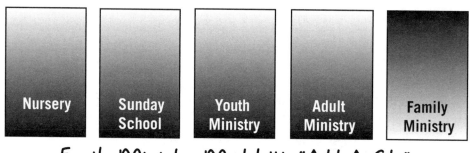

Family Ministry Model #1—"Add-A-Silo"

Silo" family ministry model. In this model the church approaches family ministry in the same way we disciple people. We take the infants and put them in nursery, we take three-year-olds through sixth graders and put them in Sunday School, we take our junior and senior high youth and put them in youth ministry, and we take our adults and put them in adult Sunday School classes or Bible studies. Each silo develops a ministry approach to grow and pass on the faith to those within its ministry.

When a church wakes up to the reality that they need to focus on families, they approach it the same way: add a silo and call it "family ministry." They put together a family ministry team and organize family game nights, family camps, family retreats, family date nights and other creative family programs. Unfortunately, even with the best of intentions and efforts these family ministry programs produce, at best, a 40 percent turnout rate. I know because I have done this myself. I have brought in some of the nation's best speakers and used every promotional tool available and we would still only see about 40 percent of our families

attend. And most of those who attended were the ones who were already passing on the faith in their homes and not the ones needing the help. What we were doing was adding another thing to an already too busy calendar of events and we weren't reaching the parents and families who truly needed to be trained and equipped to bring Christ into the center of their homes.

While the "Add-a-Silo" model is clearly the most predominant model for family ministry, because it's what we know how to do, I do not believe it is the most effective. If we want to truly advance beyond the 40 percent and bring true transformation to families, we must embrace a more integrated approach to family ministry and become churches *of* family ministry.

What Is a Church *of* Family Ministry?

For the last 25 plus years the Church has been going through a major discipleship transformation as a result of the small group ministry movement. The effectiveness of the movement within churches has been connected to the approach each church takes to small group ministry. The catch phrase

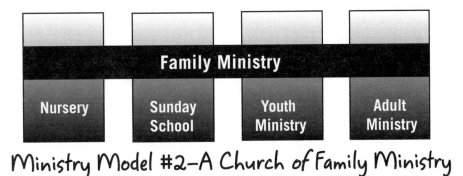

Ministry Model #2—A Church *of* Family Ministry

attached to the small group movement is, you can be a church *with* small groups or you can be a church *of* small groups. In other words, you can take a program approach to small group ministry where you add some small groups to everything else you are doing, which produces marginal impact. The other option is to make small groups an integrated part of how you do ministry as a church, exponentially increasing the transformational impact. In the same way, you can be a church *with* family ministry (the Add-a-Silo model) and have marginal impact, or you can become a church *of* family ministry where everything you do as a church is being looked at through the lenses of how we can bring Christ back into the center of every family. (See Ministry Model #2 on p.15.)

Equipping the home to be the primary place where faith is lived and nurtured should be the goal of every ministry of the church rather than just adding family ministry to the Children's Ministry Director's job description. This shouldn't be difficult for the church to embrace, as this is the way the church used to operate. Catechism was developed as an instructional tool for parents to pass on the basic teachings of the church to their children. George Barna describes it similarly in his book *Revolution*. "Christian families taught the ways of God in their homes every day. Parents were expected to model a Spirit-led lifestyle for their children, and families were to make their home a sanctuary for God. In a very real sense, the home was the early church—supplemented by larger gatherings in the

Temple and elsewhere, but never replaced by what took place in the homes of believers."[6] Therefore, in many ways, we need to go back to the way things used to be and once again reinstitute the home as the primary place where faith is nurtured.

If You "Build-It-In," They Will Come

One of the greatest challenges in family ministry is getting parents to show up for training and equipping events. No matter how great the promotion is done, how recognized the speaker is or how well-timed the event, you rarely see more than a 40 percent turnout. I know because I have tried every trick in the book myself! What if I were to say to you that there was a way to get a 98 percent turnout rate for the events that would equip parents to pass on the faith themselves? Would that peak your interest? Well, that's exactly what we were able to do and here's how.

We began by asking ourselves, *What are the faith skills that every family should be equipped to do in the home?* In other words, what does a "as for me and my household, we will serve the Lord" family look like (Joshua 24:15)? It didn't take long for us to create a healthy list of things like prayer, Bible reading, devotions, blessings, family service projects, etc. After we had compiled this list, we then went through them one by one and asked ourselves,

At what age should this faith skill be taught so it can be firmly established? For example, you probably shouldn't wait until your child is a teenager before you start the ritual of blessing them. Yet the ritual of blessing, if established before a child becomes five, can become an established ritual that can continue through the teenage years and beyond. (For a powerful example of how establishing the ritual of family blessing early can lead to rewards later read the story about Rolf Garborg and his daughter on pages 78-79 of *Faith Begins at Home.*)

Now that we had a list of faith skills we wanted to equip each family to have, and the age we thought they needed to be established, we then put together a training and equipping workshop for each faith skill. We call our family training and equipping workshops Take It Home Events (other names for these events include Faith Journey Events, Milestone Events, Faith Journey Milestone Events), and instead of putting them at another time we built them into our Sunday School and youth ministry program. When we did this, we went from a 40 percent turnout rate to 98 percent because it was much easier for parents to stick around and participate in something that they were already bringing their child to. Our parents quickly learned that at least one time per year they would be asked to go with their child to Sunday School. On that day they would be learning a new faith skill that they could start implementing in their home immediately. Over time the

Take It Home Events became a very anticipated event for families because they knew they would be receiving training that would help them as a family.

What Is a Take It Home Event?

Take It Home Events are parent-child interactive workshops where the parent(s) and child come together and learn a new faith skill that they can continue developing in the home. Take It Home Events vary in length based on a congregation's approach to children and youth ministry. A typical Take It Home Event includes worship, inspirational teaching time, interactive activity, parent-child discussion time (usually in small groups with two to three other families) and a take-home resource. The take-home resource is a critically important tool that is intended to enable the family to continue what they learned at the Take It Home Event in the home.

The purpose of each Take It Home Event is to:

- Inspire families to want to do the faith skill at home through biblical teaching and personal testimonies;
- Show families how to do the faith skill in an active learning manner that has them experience doing the faith skill together as a family; and
- Equip families to continue doing the faith skill in their home by providing a resource that will enable them to do so.

In Section 3 you will find the complete outlines for 13 Take It Home

Events beginning with an event for parents of newborns through parents of seniors in high school. Please know that these are just a few of many possible Take It Home events that can be developed and I strongly encourage you to use the input and creativity of your team to develop your own strategy for Take It Home events that will best work in your setting. I have served in four different congregations and our Take It Home strategy has looked different in each congregation. For more Take It Home ideas you can also go to the following website which was set up as a place where churches can share Take It Home Event ideas and resources: www.faithbeginsathome.com.

Before looking at the Take It Home Events there are five important keys for churches who want to make the move to becoming churches *of* family ministry.

Five Keys of Family Ministry

One of the most rewarding aspects of becoming a church *of* family ministry is the unifying momentum it creates. When I accepted the call to become the Senior Pastor of Ventura Missionary Church, I was following a great pastor who had led the church from 50 people to over 1,000 worshippers during his 25 years of leadership. One of the concerns I had, other than the fact that I

had never been a senior pastor before, was the fact that in many cases the person who follows a very successful, long-term pastor, becomes an unintentional interim pastor.

To be completely honest, after my first two years, things were headed that direction as I was burning out trying to be the pastor everyone else wanted me to be and the church was becoming frustrated trying to follow someone who was all over the place in his leadership. I remember sitting down and having a heart-to-heart with my elders to which they asked me a simple question, "What do you want to do?"

That simple question opened the floodgates for my response that once I started I quickly realized I had bottled up for too long. "If I'm going to go down, I would rather go down swinging with everything I have focused on becoming a church committed to bringing Christ back into the center of every home. My heart bleeds when I see what Satan is doing to families and we have to do something about it. I believe the church is an ocean liner riding across the ocean with the strength to stay afloat through the storms that hit. Each family is a smaller boat and from what I see, the storms are getting bigger and the majority of families are taking a beating and many of them are sinking fast. If I could do what I want, I would deploy ALL of the resources of the church into the water to rescue our families. If we only deploy one line, that won't be enough to rescue them.

We have to give it everything we have so we can bring our families back up to the surface where they can be restored and float again."

When I was done, it was like the biggest weight had been lifted from my heart and soul. I'll never forget the response of the elders. "Mark, that's why we called you here. Go for it!" And that's when the movement to become a faith-at-home-driven church began for us.

Many movements that churches go through such as starting small group ministry, beginning a contemporary or postmodern style of worship, or becoming more seeker-friendly, create disharmony and/or tension that a leader must navigate carefully through during the process. Yet the movement to become a faith-at-home-driven church is completely different. When I decided to lead the faith-at-home movement at VMC I anticipated resistance similar to when I had led churches through some of the other movements. Yet to my surprise the resistance never came. Why? Because everyone in the congregation realized that families are struggling and in need of help. The older generation had watched the disintegration of the family happen over their lifetime and they desire to see families restored. The younger generation was committed to it because they are the ones who will directly benefit from this commitment. Therefore, when a church makes a new commitment to faith at home as one of the top priorities in the church, this decision actually unites and ignites the congregation because it is something

that everyone agrees upon. As a senior pastor, I love things that create unity and positive momentum in my congregation. Therefore, the question is not "if we become faith-at-home-driven churches" but "how do we become faith-at-home-driven churches?" I believe there are five keys in becoming a faith-at-home-driven church.

KEY #1—Long-Term Commitment

If you are looking for a quick fix to transform families, you're not going to find it, and if any program you can purchase is offering it, beware. The disintegration of the family has been evolving for generations and to think it can be fixed through a 40-day program or a weekend retreat is simply not possible.

Churches need to make a long-term commitment to a model of family ministry that will train and equip families to bring Christ into their homes. Unfortunately, we do not live in a culture that is patient and persistent. We want things quickly and with as much ease as possible and if a church can't offer that for us, we will go somewhere else. Professional coaches face the reality that if they don't win a championship in the first few years they will be fired. In the same way, that's how many pastors feel as well. We look for flashy programs that will give us an instantaneous boost instead of looking at the long-term impact our ministry will make. The latest "dancing elephant" program may draw some new spectators for a period of time, but will it truly impact and equip families to make the changes that are necessary so they will be stronger 10 to 15 years from now?

I had a chance to be a part of a church, Calvary Lutheran in Golden Valley, Minnesota, that made the commitment to be a church *of* family ministry over 20 years ago. The result of this long-term commitment is that God is using Calvary to truly transform families. For example, Calvary has a large group/small group-oriented junior high ministry where they need over 60 adult small group leaders to meet with a group of 6 to 8 students every Wednesday evening. Obviously, in a normal church situation, finding 60 adults who would be willing to spend two hours every Wednesday evening with 6 to 8 squirrelly junior highers would be a very difficult task. Yet at Calvary this was not the case. In fact, in most years they had more adults willing to serve than they had openings. How did that happen?

As students registered for this program they were asked to put down the name of an adult they would like to be their small group leader. The names most requested were the student's mom and/or dad. The reason was the fact that Calvary made a commitment to training parents how to bless their infants, pray with their four-year-olds, do devotions with their first graders, read the Bible with their third graders and do service projects as an action of faith with their fifth graders. By the time they moved into the junior high program, thanks to this long-term partnership, it was no big deal for a junior high student to ask his/her parent to join them in the next step of their faith journey. Can you say countercultural? But this counterculture environment did not happen in 40 days. This is the result of 20 years of commitment.

The current family crisis did not happen overnight and the work that is needed to restore families will not happen quickly or easily. Yet a renewed commitment to faith at home is desperately needed today and if we don't start now we will simply be enabling the same behavior to continue, thereby adding to the problem. As George Barna writes in his book *Revolution*, "Unfortunately, as far as we can determine, the family will remain a mere blip on the radar screen when it comes to serving as the conduit for faith experience and expression, remaining central to perhaps five percent of the population."[7] I don't know about you, but I'm not satisfied with only five percent of families having Christ in the center of their homes and I know Christ isn't satisfied with that either. Therefore, it's time for the church to rise up and make a new commitment to family ministry or else nothing is going to change. This implementation guide is designed to help your church develop a customized, holistic model and strategy for a long-term, transformational faith at home. Family change won't happen overnight but if you make the commitment today, you will be setting a course that has the opportunity to produce results for generations to come.

SELF-ASSESSMENT QUESTIONS

1. Is your church ready to make a long-term commitment to family ministry?

2. What would you like your families to look like in 5, 10 or 15 years?

KEY #2—The Critical Role of the Senior Pastor

It is critical for the senior pastor, along with the primary leadership team of the church, to embrace the idea of becoming a faith-at-home-driven church. The senior pastor primarily determines the direction where the church will go and makes many of the staffing, teaching, budget and overall vision decisions. If equipping the home to pass on the faith is not on the radar or more importantly in the heart of the senior pastor, it will be very difficult to make some of the changes necessary to become a faith-at-home-driven church. It is important to note that senior pastors have it difficult as they have so many ministry opportunities vying for their attention. I didn't fully realize this until I became a senior pastor myself. Yet as called and appointed leaders in God's church, we must realize that the church is only as strong as the families who reside within it. As Peter Benson, Director of Search Institute,[8] stated at a conference I attended, "As the family goes so goes the future of the church. Religious life in the home is more influential than the church." I would urge senior pastors to ponder that quote for a minute and then ask the following questions: How are families going today? If the future of the church is based on how families go, then what does that say for the future of the church? If religious life in the home is more important than the church, then shouldn't we devote a majority of our time and resources to equipping the home to be the primary place where faith is nurtured?

One of the questions I frequently receive is, "How can I help my senior pastor recognize the need to become a faith-at-home-driven church?" Here are some suggestions:

- Ask your senior pastor to watch the Sr. Pastor to Sr. Pastor message given by Pastor Mark Holmen on the DVD provided as a part of this implementation guide.
- Give your senior pastor a copy of George Barna's book *Transforming Children Into Spiritual Champions* and get together once a week to discuss each chapter until you have completed the book. If you buy the breakfast or lunch you have a great chance of success!
- Give your senior pastor a copy of *Faith Begins at Home* by Mark Holmen and get together once a week to discuss each chapter until you have completed the book.
- Go through the information in this implementation guide with your senior pastor. Most senior pastors recognize the need for faith at home, they simply need a vision for how they can impact families through the existing ministries of the church.

SELF-ASSESSMENT QUESTIONS

1. Is your senior pastor committed to faith at home as one of the top priorities of the church?

2. Does your senior pastor recognize the need to be a faith-at-home-driven church?

KEY #3—Faith at Home Must Be a Part of the Mission of the Church

Every church has a mission, vision and/or strategy. For some it looks like a baseball diamond, for others it's five Gs, four Cs, or some other creative acronym. If you are going to be a faith-at-home-driven church, then faith at home must appear in your overall mission, vision and/or strategy. When I came to Ventura Missionary Church, they had already identified family as one of their core values. This was important for me since it showed me that VMC was a church that understood and embraced the critical role of the family in passing on faith to our children and children's children. As a result, when the pastoral team and I went to work creating a new mission, vision and strategy, we did so with faith at home ministry already on our radar. Take a look at how our commitment to families made its way into our mission, vision and strategy.

The mission of Ventura Missionary Church is: "To introduce people to a growing relationship with Jesus Christ."

Our vision to accomplish this mission is to continually invite people to:

- "Come and See" what a growing relationship with Christ has to offer you and your family;
- "Follow Me" and make an "as for me and my household" decision to enter into this growing relationship with Christ with a community of fellow followers;

- "Go and Be" the light of Christ in your home, community and world.
- We believe a growing relationship with Jesus Christ can be defined by four things:
    - Loving and following Jesus Christ as your personal Lord and Savior;
    - Living out faith at home;
    - Becoming connected and engaged in a local church;
    - Making a difference in the community and world.

SELF-ASSESSMENT QUESTIONS

1. Is faith at home a part of your church's mission, vision or strategy?

2. Would unchurched visitors recognize your church's commitment to them as a family?

KEY #4—Commit Resources to Faith at Home

"For where your treasure is, there your heart will be also" (Matthew 6:21). This Scripture verse can easily be adapted to apply to the church as well: "Where your budget is, so is your commitment as a church." If the church is going to make a significant impact on families, we must commit equally significant resources from our church budgets to staff and resource faith at home. Unfortunately, what I have seen in most churches is that a large percentage of the budget is spent on programs and resources that will be used primarily at church, yet scarcely any funds are spent on resources that the family can use in the home.

Take a look at your current church budget and ask, "How much money are we spending as a church to equip the home to be the primary place where faith is nurtured?" If the home is more influential than the church, as statistics have shown, then shouldn't we be devoting more resources to what is more effective and God ordained?

When I served as the Youth and Family Ministry Pastor at Calvary Lutheran Church in Golden Valley, Minnesota, we were spending as much money in our children's ministry on resources that we would give away at our Take It Home Events to be used in the home as we were on Sunday School curriculum. Obviously, this was a major commitment that took many years to build up, so when I came to serve as the Senior Pastor of Ventura Missionary Church I knew that we would need to increase our financial commitment to faith at home. On one Sunday I gave a sermon entitled "Home as Church Too," based on Deuteronomy 6, and during the message I painted a picture of some of the things we wanted to do to equip parents to pass on the faith to their children. In the message I also informed the congregation that these ideas needed financial support that was not in our budget. I concluded the message by giving the congregation a chance to make a one-Sunday, above and beyond, finan-

cial gift to our new faith at home effort. The congregation responded with over $30,000, which became the seed money we needed to fund our new faith at home efforts until we could build it into our annual budget.

SELF-ASSESSMENT QUESTIONS

1. What percentage of your church budget is devoted to faith at home?

2. What percentage of your budget is committed to providing resources families/individuals can use in the home?

KEY #5—Get All Ministries Involved

A common mistake that I have seen is that churches pigeonhole family ministry under the umbrella of Children's Ministry. This ends up adding a huge responsibility to an already overextended ministry and it prevents other ministries from taking an active role in transforming families.

When family ministry is appropriately elevated to being a part of how you "do" church, it becomes something that every ministry can get involved in. Women's ministry can help women pass on the faith in the home; men's ministry can help men do the same. The seniors ministry can help seniors play an active role in mentoring younger families because seniors are the last generation that remembers what it was like to have prayer, devotions and Bible reading as a part of your home life. Small group ministry can help families get connected with other families who are experiencing for the first time what it's like to have Christ in the center of their homes and outreach ministry can help families get engaged in serving others in your community. Limiting family ministry to children's ministry is a disservice to your families and your church.

One of the most common questions I receive is, "How do I get all of the ministries engaged in this commitment to being a faith-at-home-driven church?" One of the best ways I have discovered to get broader support for family ministry is to have a one-day family ministry summit meeting. (A family ministry summit meeting outline can be found on page 43.) The purpose of a family ministry summit meeting is to share the biblical mandate for family ministry and create a sense of urgency and ownership for becoming a faith-at-home-driven church through ALL the ministries of your congregation.

For example, in one congregation I served the results of our family ministry summit meeting led to our men's ministry making Faith Chests®—wood

boxes that looked like small hope chests, which were given to the parents of each child that was dedicated. Not to be outdone, the women's ministry gave nighttime devotional tapes to the parents on the one-year anniversary of the child's dedication and the quilting group made baby quilts for the child. The singles' ministry decided they wanted to give Bibles to the family of every third grader and help parents pass on a tradition of Bible memorization to their children and the youth ministry team decided they would put together a retreat where they would help parents and teens talk about sexuality (Dating, Kissing, Sex & Stuff). The summit meeting served as a catalyst for our journey towards becoming a faith-at-home-driven church as each ministry now had a part to play in making the vision happen.

SELF-ASSESSMENT QUESTIONS

1. Do the other ministries of your church recognize the role they play in family ministry?

2. Are the other ministries of your church equipping the home to be the primary place where faith is nurtured?

KEY QUESTIONS FOR CONSIDERATION

1. Is your church ready to make a long-term commitment to faith at home, recognizing that there is no quick fix for the transformation that needs to occur within families?

2. Is your senior pastor committed to making faith at home one of the top priorities in your church?

3. Is faith at home integrated into the mission, vision and strategy of your church?

4. Has your church made the financial commitment necessary to becoming a faith-at-home-driven church?

5. Are all the ministries of the church incorporated and committed to your faith at home efforts?

Notes

1. George Barna, *Transforming Children into Spiritual Champions* (Ventura, CA: Regal Books, 2003), pp. 83-84.

2. Ibid., pp. 93-94.

3. Reprinted with permission from Effective Christian Education: *A National Study of Protestant Congregations.* Copyright 1990 by Search Institute. No other use is permitted without prior permission from Search Institute, 615 First Avenue NE, Minneapolis, MN 55413 www.search-institute.org.

4. Tom Schultz, *Group Magazine* (Group Publishers, 1995).

5. Dr. Roland Martinson serves as the professor of pastoral care and theology at Luther Seminary in St. Paul, Minnesota. The Youth and Family Institute is a nonprofit organization that presents a partnership of family and congregation in which the home is viewed as the primary place for teaching and nurturing the faith through conferences, consultation, training, and development of publications and practical resources for pastors, youth educators and church professionals. Website: www.youthandfamilyinstitute.org.

6. George Barna, *Revolution* (Carol Stream, IL: Tyndale House Publishers, 2006), p. 24.

7. Ibid., p. 49.

8. Search Institute is a nonprofit, nonsectarian research and educational organization that advances the well-being and positive development of children and youth through applied research, evaluation, consultation, training, and the development of publications and practical resources for educators, youth-serving professionals, parents, community leaders and policy makers. Phone: 1-800-888-7828. Website: www.search-institute.org.

Section 2

Getting Started

As you prepare to get started in training families, you will want to review three additional tools that will help you launch the movement in your congregation. First, in this section, you will find some very enlightening insights from Pastor Dave Teixeira, Youth and Family Ministry Pastor who has had to build the model from the ground up at Ventura Missionary Church in Ventura, California. Dave will address many of the questions and concerns you will potentially face as you lead your church to become a faith-at-home-driven church.

A second tool that has been provided in this section is a Faith at Home Leadership Summit outline. A Faith at Home Leadership Summit is an event that brings together all the staff and lay leaders of your church to build unity and passion for becoming a church that is committed to reestablishing the home as the primary place where faith is nurtured. At the end of the summit, the leaders of your church will understand the need for becoming a faith-at-home-driven church and the role they will play in making it happen.

And finally, a third tool is a five-week Faith Begins at Home Sermon Series (see p. 217) that can help build congregational support. The Faith Begins at Home Sermon Series is founded on Mark Holmen's book, *Faith Begins at Home* which can be the basis for a great small group series. *Faith Begins at Home* includes small group discussion questions at the end of each chapter so that your church can incorporate or launch small groups during the five-week sermon series. The sermon series is in outline form with Power Point slides on the DVD bound into this implementation guide. Customize the slides to your situation. May the Lord bless you as you begin the journey toward becoming a church *of* family ministry!

Building It from the Ground Up

**Insights from
Pastor Dave Teixeira,
Youth and Family Ministry Pastor**

Up-Front Encouragement

UP-FRONT

honest, candid; straightforward; initial investment; in advance; beforehand; direct; forthright; genuine.

If you look up the word "up-front" in a dictionary or thesaurus, you will find a list of words that describe the goal of this section of your implementation guide. In other words, here are some honest, candid, straightforward, forthright, direct, genuine initial insights you will need to know in advance, that is, before you take the empowering families plunge.

The Ultimate Goal

One thing about the Take It Home approach is that we must really understand our goals if we want to be successful. You see, most of the time, our measuring stick for success in the church is the impact, intensity, excitement or fun that we feel during an event.

• How enthusiastically did the kids sing at VBS?

• How much discussion was there about the Bible story in the small group?
• Were the kids really engaged and listening during the story?

These are great questions, but not the ultimate question for Take It Home Events. Should our events be fun, exciting, engaging, filled with passion and energy? YES! However, the big question does not center on the event itself. The rubber meets the road when the families go home. What happens in the home as the result of your event is what we must evaluate ourselves on. Want to know if your events are effective? Don't ask if parents enjoyed the story, activity or music. Ask if they are implementing devotions, prayer or service into their routines at home with their kids. If your event seemed pretty average but Dad is doing nighttime devotions with his daughter, or Mom is praying with the kids before breakfast or your families are now serving together once a month in the community, score yourself an A+ and take the day off, you deserve it!

Nurture Their Nature

Recently I was reading a book on understanding yourself that was based on the Myers-Briggs Type Indicator. You probably know that Myers-Briggs is a personality test that identifies a person's individual preferences or characteristics. However, the author of the book I was reading made the staggering point that personality is made up of two components. The first is temperament, a configuration of predisposed inclinations. The second is character, a configuration of learned habits and disciplines. In other words, children are born with a temperament given to them by God that we cannot and would not want to change. However, we have an amazing opportunity and responsibility to take the unique temperament of each child and overlay it with the character of God by instilling habits and disciplines that will keep them connected to Christ. This is ultimately what this entire manual is about. It is about recognizing that parents have the most power and influence over the habits and disciplines formed in their children. Thus, we must empower parents to successfully overlay Christ-connecting habits into the lives of their children. When this happens, our children will truly grow up to become all that God desires they will be.

Help Your Parents See into Future Generations!

We all know from personal experience that much of what we do in our homes is the result of what we grew up with. Dad read the paper every morning at the table while drinking a cup of coffee before work. Why? Because that's what Dads do. We open one Christmas gift on Christmas Eve and the rest on Christmas morning. Why? Because that's how my parents did it with me when I was a kid. For Thanksgiving we eat that green-bean casserole with cream of mushroom soup in it. Why? Mom made that dish every year for Thanksgiving. We could all come up

with thousands of other examples of how we do things because it is the way they were done in our homes growing up. Quite often we don't even realize that this is the reason we do certain things. They are so much a part of who we are that we just do them without a second thought.

Here's where the huge opportunity comes in! Your families start praying, blessing, doing devotions, serving and worshiping together on a regular basis and those kids will grow up to not only do those things themselves, but also to do them with their kids. Why? Because it will subconsciously become who they are ("Because that's what we always did at my house and that's just what families do, isn't it?"). See the big picture here? Your tiny little event could impact not just a kid, not just one family, but families, children and people for generations to come! Cast that vision to your parents and watch them get excited as they realize the power of the opportunity you are placing in their hands.

Discipling Parents Through their Kids!

How many times have we heard about people coming BACK to church once they've had kids? It's true; kids are a wonderful evangelism tool for the church and ultimately the Kingdom of God. But, all too often, churches don't leverage children as a tool for the discipleship of parents. After the parents are in the doors, we instantly separate them from their children and try to entice them into an adult specific discipleship program. The problem is that in the same way the parents weren't motivated to come to church before kids, they aren't motivated to come to an extra church program just for themselves. Remember, they came for their kids, not themselves. And this is one of the beauties of these events. Under the guise of something good for your kids or family, we are ultimately able to teach parents about incorporating spiritual disciplines into, not only the lives of their children, but into their lives as well. Think about prayer, for example. What you are teaching about prayer is at the kindergarten level; it's step one basic stuff. But realistically, this is exactly what most of our parents need. And because "it's for the kids," many adults will personally begin to engage God through prayer for the first time at home. Then add to the list family worship, devotions, service, Scripture reading and more. If that's not discipleship, I don't know what is!

Culture Change

CULTURE

the behaviors, beliefs and characteristics of a particular social, ethnic, or age group that have been ingrained through training, experience, perception and practice.

Helping your families see that their home is the primary place where faith is nurtured is a significant shift in thinking. In fact, it flies in the face of the behaviors, beliefs and characteristics that have been ingrained in your people through training, experience, perception and practice.

An Uphill Battle

One thing I love about airports is those moving sidewalks. You can just be sauntering along when, all of a sudden, you look over and you're flying with little effort at maximum speed. It's a great scenario! Unfortunately, this will not be your experience trying to get families to own their responsibility for passing on the faith to their children. I wish it was. I wish I could tell you to just jump in the river and that the current would sweep you away downstream. I wish I could say, "Just get the ball rolling and things will take care of themselves." I guess I could tell you all of that, but it would be a lie. The reality is that if you take seriously the call to empower families, it will be an uphill climb. Not only does our society create roadblocks for families but, over the past 40 years even our church culture has consistently abdicated the faith-passing responsibility of parents, and changing that mindset will not be easy.

But surprisingly, if you challenge the underlying belief in most families and congregations that church is the place where kids learn about faith in Christ, you won't encounter an out-and-out rebellion. No, it will be worse. You'll encounter passive resistance. People won't argue with you, throw temper tantrums or speak out against your efforts at church council meetings.

Instead, they will just passively not engage. They might even have a good attitude and great intentions but they have been heavily influenced by a culture that teaches them to drop off their children for faith, and culture is hard to change. Think about our American society and how ingrained outsourcing our kids has become. If we want our kids to:

- Learn piano, we take them to piano lessons;
- Learn soccer, we sign them up for the soccer team;
- Learn karate, we drop them off at karate lessons;
- Learn to dance, we enroll them at a dance studio.

Know from the beginning that although it may not seem like a big change, you are fighting years of American and church culture and it will take some time for the shift to occur!

Be a Broken Record!

In order to fight the prevailing culture your families need to hear a consistent, continual message from you reminding and encouraging them as they attempt to go where very few other families and churches have gone before. Use every opportunity. Will your people get tired of hearing it? I hope so, but send a message! Say it again and again. What again is that message? "It's up to you. We can't do it without you. The opportunity is amazing and you can do it. We are here to help in whatever way we can. Our role is to support and reinforce what happens in your home." Say it however you want to, but say it, and say it often.

Your Church Is from Missouri— SHOW Them!

One of my buddies is famous for making a statement and following it up by saying, "That and $5 will buy you a cup of coffee at Starbucks." This tells us that we can't just talk about empowering families, we must SHOW people how serious we are.

One way of showing your church that faith in the home is a priority is by preaching about it. Everyone knows that the most influential and important place of communication in the Church is the pulpit. If families living out their faith is the topic of an entire sermon, people will see the value your church places on what happens in their home. If there are several sermons, the congregation will really take notice. The last section of this implementation guide gives five sermon ideas that can be used as a series, or periodically over the course of several months or years.

Time is another very concrete and practical way of showing your congregation that the home is where it's at. We spend our time doing what we care and are passionate about. People know this. And so if they hear you talking a lot about the home but see you spending 99 percent of your energy planning church programs for kids, your words and $5 will buy you a cup of coffee at Starbucks! Spend time and energy on empowering families. This may mean that something else has to end, but your time and energy will make a statement to your people and they will notice! Planning and implementing some of the Take It Home Events outlined in this implementation guide is a great first step!

Finally, you must show your congregation that you are committed to the home through resources. All churches have limited resources and often we have to make tough decisions about how we will use those resources to move the Kingdom of God forward through our ministries. When parents see significant portions of church resources (and this includes staffing) being used to empower what is happening in their homes, it will make a significant statement to them about what you really believe in and the expectations you have of them as parents and families. Investing quality resources in your families will send a strong message that won't soon be forgotten. With each Take It Home Event found in this implementation guide we have listed suggested resources you can send home with your families. Some cost more than others but no matter what the cost, you will make a statement when you put tools in the hands of your families.

You Say You Want an Evolution?

EVOLUTION

a process of gradual, peaceful, growth and development resulting in transformation.

Don't rework your entire ministry. Most if not all of what you are currently doing is wonderful ministry for kids. The goal of this book is to help you with the process of gradual, peaceful, growth and development that will result in the transformation of your families from the inside out.

I was lucky enough to play college basketball at Hastings College (a private school in Nebraska—Go Broncos!). Despite being a small school, we had a history of basketball tradition and both our coach and team took very seriously being the best we could as we represented HC on the court. So for four years, as a part of the team, I spent countless hours practicing and working on my game. But even with all the energy and effort, there were times when it seemed I wasn't really improving all that much. Then one day, shortly after my senior season had wrapped up, I played one-on-one with a buddy who I happened to have played against four years earlier. At Hastings College on a football scholarship, he was a great athlete. I remembered him being a good basketball player and recalled just barely beating him in a game long ago. Well, this game was a completely different story! I not only beat him, I skunked him. He didn't score a single point! After the game ended he said, "Man, you've really gotten a lot better!" And that was when I realized how much all those hours really HAD improved my game. It wasn't that noticeable along the way, but now looking back, it was as clear as day.

The same will be true of your ministry to empower families. Three months from now you aren't going to notice a dramatic difference in all or even a few of the families and children in your church. Take It Home Events aren't a magic formula that will create instantaneous results. If that is what you are looking for, you won't find it here. What you will find here is an approach to family ministry that will slowly, and almost undetectably, transform families from the inside out over the course of many years. This is not a diet pill promising to get you into your old high school prom dress in two weeks. Empowering the home is going to be like the hours of work required by anything worth having. You have to believe in it. You have to trust that it will and is working. But most importantly, you have to know it is right!

New Lenses

I have worn glasses ever since I was in first grade. For me it was no big deal, because I actually liked my glasses. My Dad wore glasses as well and it was kind of something we shared. "The best looking people wear glasses," he'd say. It made me feel good. Unfortunately, up through my college years I had no fashion sense when it came to my glasses. Looking back at pictures I can hardly believe how HUGE my frames actually were. *How could my nose hold the weight of those enormous things?* Then one day, after being married a few months, my wife said, "Let's get you some new glasses." Looking at my glasses, I agreed that it was time for an

upgrade. Amy picked out several sleek designer frames for me to try on. "How much are these?" I asked. She gave me "the look" and I slipped them on and glanced in the mirror. *Wow, what a difference. I looked hip!* Such a small change and I felt like a whole new guy.

The same thing can happen in your ministry, if you will look at what you're doing through some new lenses. Faith in the home does not require a major overhaul of all your current programming. Start by simply taking a look at what you're currently doing through the lens of empowering the home. You're probably doing more than you think and with some minor changes you can begin to shift your focus. Let me give you an example.

Lions and Tigers and Sex, Oh My!

When I started in youth ministry, one of the first assignments I received was to lead an overnight retreat with eighth graders centered on the topic of sex and sexuality. Fun! No seriously, my thinking was that if anything was going to capture the attention of these squirrelly, hormone-driven little beasts, it was going to be sex. I began putting together my game plan. The first year the retreat ran pretty well. The next year, as I added material, became more seasoned as a youth worker and figured out what the kids needed to hear, the retreat began to take off. By year three it was a well-oiled machine that was really making a difference in the lives of the kids who came. We had honesty, confession, repentance, decisions and tears. It was a powerful weekend. I came home feeling like a champion. The next Sunday morning I strolled through the church lobby like a king anticipating the many parents who would come rushing up to thank me for the impact I had made on their child. They never came. Finally, I began to ask specific parents whose kids I knew had been deeply moved over the weekend. "How did Johnny's retreat go?" "What did Sally say about the weekend?" "Did Lisa tell you about the long talk we had?" The responses were virtually identical as one after another, parents told me that their kids had said very little if anything to them about what had gone on. That's when it hit me. We were not empowering parents to teach and guide their kids through the difficult years of sexual development. In fact, we had done exactly the opposite. We had literally taken the kids away from Mom and Dad, had an experience with them and had made no effort to connect our retreat with the home. With our vast understanding of youth culture, our game plan seemed to be that eighth graders would simply go home and spend endless hours talking with there parents, recounting all the details of the powerful weekend. OK, we blew it! Something had to change.

We didn't throw out the retreat. In fact, we didn't change any of the material we covered over the weekend. We simply began to think about how we could include Mom and Dad in this process while keeping an open, unhindered atmosphere with the kids—not an

easy combo. Finally, we decided on our new plan of attack. Near the end of the retreat (located about an hour away) I would drive back early to meet with the parents back at the church. I would spend a couple hours with them talking about what we had covered at the retreat, giving them an overview of what eighth graders think, feel and face when it comes to sex, and talking to them about their important role as parents. Then, after having the parents all to myself, the kids would return and join us. After the "been away for a night" greeting, parents and kids would sit together and I would lead them through a discussion. (See Take It Home Event "Talking About Dating, Kissing, Sex & Stuff" on pp. 168-210 for more info on creating a comfortable atmosphere during the discussion.) Then we would send them off with resources and homework to do together that included a two-page list of questions to help create dialogue.

So, how did it go? I was finally king of the church lobby (not the ultimate goal, but appreciation when you work with eighth graders is something to relish). Parents came up to me in droves to thank me and talk about the impact the retreat had had on their family. Not only did parents and kids have long, intense discussions about sex, but it turns out that this conversation opened the door for other discussions about middle school life as well. I guess if you can talk to your eighth grader about sex, you can talk about anything. Several years later, doing the same retreat, but this time in a new church, I stood in the back of the room during our closing session with parents and kids. As I stood there watching the interactions between mothers and fathers and sons and daughters, a volunteer came up to me and said one word, "Money!" She was right. When the church empowers parents to engage with their kids instead of trying to do it for them, it is like "money" in the bank, and once again it was payday!

You'll Get Better

"What just happened?" I thought as I left church one morning. I never thought I would get my rear whooped by a bunch of two-year-olds, but I just had. It was our first Take It Home Event for twos and their parents on Family Blessings. We had a great morning planned—food, music, a puppet show and even a little set portraying a child's bedroom where we would show parents what blessing your child each night before bed might look like. Feeling like the parents would want some Bible exposition on the theology behind blessing, I had come prepared with about 10 minutes of teaching on the subject. Then we would get practical and begin helping parents write and practice blessing their own children. For some reason (and this is surprising because at the time I had a two-year-old) in my mind the two-year-olds were going to sit quietly in Mommy and Daddy's laps while I talked peacefully with the parents about the history and theology of blessing. You know what happened instead? Kids were every-

where! Moms were up and chasing, Dads were frustrated and I literally could not get through one sentence without a major interruption. I felt like we had failed.

But here's the point. We hadn't failed! First of all, several parents from that group told me later that they had begun blessing their children and one father told me that his daughter won't go to sleep without his blessing her first. (Again, the goal isn't how well the event goes!) Second, and most importantly, we had learned. Following the event we went right to work evaluating and brainstorming how we might change the format for next time to help things run smoother. And you know what, things DID run smoother!

This year we tried our first Computer Savvy Parents Take It Home Event for parents of middle school and high school students. It was just OK. Honestly, I gave the event a D+ (I'm a hard grader). However, I promise you that next year's event will be better because we learned so much this first time. During the question-and-answer time we learned what kinds of questions parents will ask. Watching parents and kids interact, we discovered where the tension points between parents and kids lie. We found out how much time it takes to do a virtual tour of the Internet and what parents want most in terms of filtering info. So, despite our D+ this year, the event was a success and a step in the right direction. Next year I'm anticipating at least a B.

Skeptical Questions

SKEPTICISM

disbelief; doubting, testing, questioning attitude or state of mind

So, you don't really believe it? You have a questioning state of mind that keeps asking how these simple events could possibly transform the faith lives of kids and families? Well, you're not the first one to ask the hard questions. Hopefully, this section will give you some insights into our thinking and help relieve some of your skepticism.

Just One One-Hour Event a Year? Are You Kidding?

Inevitably, whenever we tell people about our big approach to transforming families and homes for Christ we will get asked a question that goes something like this. "So, you are telling me that the Johnsons, who have one third-grade son, will be transformed by coming to one Sunday School hour this year where we talk about the Bible? I mean, it doesn't seem like you're doing that much." GREAT question, and the answer is you are absolutely correct! You're NOT doing that much! That is the beautiful part of the whole approach; it's not about you. This program isn't about us giving you (already busy and maxed out children's ministry director, youth pastor, Sunday school teacher) more work to do. It is about us empowering par-

ents to do the work they can and should be doing in the home. Let's go back to the Johnsons. Their son Timmy is in a class with six other children, and of the seven families, let's say six (the Wilsons are out of town—too bad!) show up to your Take It Home Event about the Bible. You spend one hour encouraging and equipping them to read the Scriptures together and send them home with a resource or two. And let's say half (for all you pessimists out there) actually begin applying that faith skill in their homes on an average of (again for you pessimists) four times a week. If you do the math, that is 624 times over the next year that your families will be engaged with one another and God through His Word! And it only took you one hour! Multiply that over the next seven years of that child's life and you have just done something pretty major. Not convinced? Let's look at it from one more angle. You do five Take It Home Events for kids from preschool through the eighth grade. So now, the Johnsons have been empowered to do five things with Timmy over the years. And, choosing at random, let's say they have been a part of the following Take It Home Events:

- Baby Dedication (with godparents)
- Family Devotions
- Prayer
- My Bible
- Computer Boundaries

So now as an 18-year-old going off to college:

- Tim has a relationship with an adult couple who, several times a year, connect with and encourage Tim in his walk with the Lord;

- Tim devotes specific quality time with the Lord about five days a week;
- Tim spends time daily in prayer and Bible reading;
- With the help of Mom and Dad, Tim has managed to steer clear of negative computer influences.

Is this kid prepared to live for Christ out on his own? More so than he would be without that list. But he and his family only spent five hours of church programming? I'll bet it means much more than that to Tim!

How Much Do Families Have Time For?

As you look down the list of Take It Home Events, you can easily start to feel as if Mom and Dad could get overwhelmed. In theory, if you stick just to our list, by the time the child is a sixth grader, parents will be: blessing their children, leading family devotions, praying, serving, worshiping, and reading the Bible regularly with their children. Great, but when are families going to have time together for all that? Have you seen family schedules lately? Yes, it can be a lot. But here's why this plan will still work.

First, not every family is going to connect with every event. Some families will really get into blessing their kids and having family worship time. Other families will connect by reading Scripture together. Other families will love serving and praying as a family. If every Take It Home event does not infiltrate the rou-

tine of every family's daily life, it's OK. I think if families engaged in two or three of the things you are teaching on a regular basis, that alone could change the lives of children and families for generations to come. Again, consider the fact that many if not most of your families are currently doing NONE of the things we want to empower them to do.

Second, both parents don't have to do everything with the kids together. Obviously it is great for kids to have attention from both parents, but sometimes individual attention can be just as needed and can create a special bond between that parent and child. What if Dad's routine was to give the kids a bath or tuck them into bed every night and at the same time do devotions with them? What if Mom, after waking the kids up, started every day by praying for and with each child? I can hear it now, "When I was a kid my Dad did devotions with us every night. I'll never forget that." Or, "Starting the day with Mom praying for me helped me feel so loved and ready to face the day with God at my side." Maybe these roles can switch from time to time and the family can serve or worship all together on a less frequent basis. But the point is, families can and will make the time if you help them make it a priority.

Building Momentum (A Special Section for Children's Pastors/Directors)

Where and how will you find the energy, force, impulse, thrust, impetus and drive to move the home forward in the awareness of your church? How can you get the ball rolling in the right direction? How much influence do you really need from the top?

Can You Do It Without the Senior Pastor?

Would it be great if the senior pastor was on board with your vision to empower families to live the faith out in their homes? Yes. Would it be great to have sermons about the importance of investing in our children frequently come from the pulpit of your church? Definitely. And would it be nice to feel like the children, youth and family budget and staffing were a high priority to the leadership of your church? Absolutely. But here's the reality. I know Pastor Mark says at the beginning of this implementation guide that, "It is critically important for the senior pastor . . . to embrace the idea of becoming a church *of* family ministry," but in your church this may or may not happen. And furthermore, you may not have any control over this. But you can do it anyway. Yes, little old you, the one with the half-office in the back corner of the church basement. I hate to say this, but my coauthor is a senior pastor, and to tell you something you already know, senior pastors can be a bit narcissistic. They think if they don't start it, support it or promote it, it won't happen. I love you, Mark, but it's not always true! The Take It Home Events outlined in this implementation guide are very easily begun with little money and support from the bigwigs of your congregation, including

the senior pastor. Now, I'm not saying to do anything in secrecy, or even under the radar of your pastor. However, even without your pastor doing cartwheels, you can begin to move forward. Just let the appropriate people know you are going to start some training events for families and get started. Start small, build a team of people with a similar passion and watch it grow. In a few years, when enough momentum has grown, you had better believe the senior pastor will get on board (and probably take all the credit for your work)!

Church Size

I think there is such a thing as critical mass. So if you are from a smaller church, you may have to combine some ages for your events. There are some challenges with this but it can definitely work and the energy and excitement you gain by having more families participate is worth the extra work.

If you are combining age groups, there are some things you can do to help the event work for the multiple ages:

- Have separate age-appropriate resources;
- Have table groups formed by age of the children;
- Have the families partner by age of children to discuss implementation ideas;
- When appropriate in the training, give tips for working with older and younger children.

For Parents or Kids?

One conflict we have run into at our Take It Home Events is teaching and training the parents while at the same time holding the attention of the children. This can be especially challenging with younger children who have not yet learned to sit still and listen. There are two approaches we have adopted to solve this problem and both can and have worked.

Approach 1—Keep Kids Separate for the Teaching

This approach seeks to solve the problem by starting the event with the kids in a separate room from the parents. The kids, for example, may be in their usual Sunday School room with the teacher while the parents gather in the Take It Home Event room for adult level teaching and training. Then after the adults have been given the information they need, the kids come in for the experiential part of the event and the adults can apply the training they have received with the children now present and engaged. This works well in situations where there is a high level of parental training needed for a particular faith skill and the kids have a short attention span and cannot sit through this section. You may want to consider using this approach in the Family Blessings event for two-year-olds and their families. You may want 10 minutes to help your adults understand what, why and how to bless their children, and two-year-olds present in the room during that time could prevent

parents from giving you their full attention. Kids apart works great for this event.

Approach 2—Train Together

This approach seeks to solve the problem by using various training techniques to engage the children while training the parents to successfully apply the faith skill. It is my opinion that, if possible, this approach is the option to go with. However, you may have to make both time and content sacrifices in order to keep the children engaged and prevent them from becoming a disruption to the training. A great example of this approach is found in our Family Devotions Event outline for three-year-olds. By using the "Bag O' Success" and keeping the training tips to short sound bites, you can train your adults and keep your three-year-olds engaged at the same time. While you may have to sacrifice your 10-minute mini-sermon on the biblical foundations of devotions, your parents will appreciate the way you model keeping the program on the same level as the kids and they will hopefully apply that same principle when doing their own devotions at home!

Selling Your Youth Staff!

Whether or not the senior pastor of your church buys into the vision to empower families or not, one important group to get on board is the youth staff of your church. There is nothing worse than watching years of building into children and families completely drop off when kids move on to junior high. Show your youth pastor what you have done (or intend to do) in children's ministry, the changes you have implemented, the impact it has made and brainstorm how this approach might look with the youth. Don't come in with it all planned out, allow the youth pastor to be a part of the brainstorming process so he or she has some ownership. Start first by asking the youth pastor to read "You Say You Want an Evolution?" and "New Lenses" on pages 32-33. Show the youth pastor the events for teens we have outlined in this implementation guide, and even offer to help with the events. If your youth pastor is uninterested, you may have to begin with some lay leaders or parents that are active in your youth department.

Teen Mania

MANIA

excessive excitement; intense enthusiasm; craze; interest; desire.

When you tell your kids that you are inviting their parents to join you for the final part of your sex retreat, I can't promise that your announcement will be met with excitement, enthusiasm or even interest. But if you commit to empowering parents, I promise that your students will warm up, your parents will be forever grateful, and there will be a new enthusiasm for teens in your church community.

But the Kids Don't Want Their Parents There, and I Don't Either!

Elementary-aged children are in a phase where they are determining what they believe. But as kids move into their teen years, they are determining how they will live and who they will become. They are asking questions like, "How will what I believe direct and determine the decisions I make?" Youth pastors, you have both the biggest challenge and the biggest opportunity. Everyone expects parents to be involved with their kids when they are in elementary school. It's a given. But when they hit junior high both kids and parents are looking for "space."

"You want me to bring my parents to youth group? Are you kidding?"

"Jason's mother and I have talked it over and we've been involved with him up at church since he was little. So, we have decided to let him be influenced by some other adults now. That just seems to be what he needs." However, while some space for kids this age can be healthy, the gap can grow pretty wide pretty fast and parents will soon be searching for connecting points. If you can create a periodic venue for parents and kids to connect, talk and work out key adolescent issues you will not only be a hero, but you will be much more effective in helping your students determine who they will be and how they will live as Christ-followers in this crazy world.

Making It Work With Teens

Programs ALWAYS look different when you transfer them from the child-world to the youth-world. So how might the Take It Home approach look in a youth ministry context? Your primary goal is the same as that of your children's ministry co-workers: to empower the parents to pass on the faith. How can this work best? I honestly believe the Take It Home program can work with kids of all ages when you apply the principles in a way that fits your group. Consider the size of your group, who the kids are, what they are facing in life and then adapt Take It Home to work for your group. Here are a few ideas to get your thoughts going:

• Should I have an event for each age group? If your class sizes are big enough, plan an event for each age group. However, this may not always be necessary. As the kids get older, it becomes easier to teach on subjects that span several grade levels. Plus, in many youth situations, kids are used to being grouped together with several age groups. But don't get too overzealous and try to run seven events the first year. I would suggest starting with an event or two for junior highers and the same for senior high. (You could do an event for upper grades and lower grades as you get started in high school.)

• Should parents be a part of the entire event? Not necessarily. With teens I often find that having a separate time for them and their parents before bringing them together works

well. First, it provides a warm-up time to get conversation rolling. Second, it allows for a level of candor from both groups that may never happen when you mix the two.

• What subjects will work for teens? You can probably tell from the events listed in this implementation guide that as kids get older, events focus more on specific life issues and choices that kids will make. I alluded to the reason for this earlier when I talked about where teens are in the developmental process. Right now in their life these kids are trying to figure out how all the things they have been taught in Sunday School translate into their life. Choose issues your kids are facing so that you can empower Mom and Dad to help them work out how their relationship with Christ directs the choices they make in these areas. Your program will not only connect kids and parents, and provide biblical direction for those specific issues, but also show them how their Christian worldview impacts even the most sensitive areas of their lives. By helping kids and parents recognize this with several issues, you will also be modeling a process they can apply to other areas of their life.

• Will parents really show up? So how do you actually get parents to show up for these events? How is this any different than getting parents to show up to help out on a normal youth group night? Well, you're going to have to work at it! BUT there are two primary differences working in your favor. First, you are only asking them to show for a single isolated event. And second, you are not asking them to connect with or engage the (very scary and intimidating) teen population in general, just their kid. But will that do it? Sorry, but no. My experience tells me that a general, "Parents come with your kids to youth group next Wednesday" announcement will not be effective if you announce it in youth group for a month prior, print it in the bulletin and youth newsletter, and have the pastor preach an entire sermon on it. The "anti-parent doing anything faith-related with teens" culture is much too established for anything less than an all-out assault. I suggest requiring your students to sign up for these events and making parental attendance part of the sign up process. But what if a child's parent is unable or unwilling to come? A substitute adult will do in this case (uncle, grandparent, friend, adult youth volunteer, etc.). Let me once again use Talking About Dating, Kissing, Sex & Stuff Take It Home Event as an example. First, we pique the kids' interest by using the words "sex" and "stuff" in the title. How

can they resist? Next, we entice the parents to sign up their kids using out-and-out fear tactics. (Kidding, kind of!) Then, when they call to sign up, we REQUIRE parental attendance. We also get contact information for parents and not only remind them of their commitment, but also make sure they have a clear picture of their child sitting alone while all the other kids are feeling loved because they have a parent sitting next to them. (This would never happen, but the image is very effective!) In all sincerity, we communicate clearly that the parental portion is NOT OPTIONAL. If you communicate this to the parents (not just the kids), you will actually be surprised at the parental turnout, especially if you are addressing relevant topics.

I hope by now that I've convinced you about the huge impact that Take It Home Events can have on the spiritual growth of families (and everyone!) in your church. It's manageable! It's doable! And it's worth every penny and every effort. To get started, plan now when you can take the first step: the Faith at Home Leadership Summit. The outline begins on the next page

Faith at Home Leadership Summit Outline

Corresponding PowerPoint slides are available on the DVD provided with this implementation guide.

I. Opening: Create an Inviting Atmosphere

A. Food, decorations, music playing, name tags, etc.

B. Have people sit at round tables in their ministry teams. For example:

1. Table 1—Music and worship leaders (lay and staff)

2. Table 2—Adult ministry leaders (men's ministry, women's ministry, etc.)

3. Table 3—Children's ministry leaders

4. Table 4—Youth ministry leaders

5. Table 5—Elders/general board

C. Begin by thanking people for giving their most precious commodity—their time—to participate in this summit meeting.

II. Time of Worship (30 minutes)

A. Take time to refuel your leaders through a time of praise and worship.

B. Pray for the Holy Spirit to come and give your team unity and vision for a family ministry that will transform the lives of families in your community.

C. Add your own worship slides.

III. Session I: What Are We Accomplishing? (60 minutes)

A. *Opening discussion starter:* Before we get started, an important point to note is that when you use the word "family," you are talking about every form of family. A single person in a nursing home is a form of family, a dual income no kids (DINK) couple is a form of family, etc.

1. Tell the audience that a *USA Today* article once stated that there were over 28 forms of family.

2. State that when you say the word "family," you will be talking about *all* 28 forms of family.

3. Share the following quote from Peter Benson, Director of Search

Institute: "As the family goes so goes the future of the church. Religious life in the home is more influential than the church."[1]

B.   As a group, discuss the following questions:

1. How are families in our church and community going today?

2. If this is the future of the Church, what does that mean for our church?

3. Do you agree that religious life in the home is more influential than the Church? Why or why not?

C.   In a national survey by Search Institute titled "The Most Significant Religious Influences," teenagers were asked to identify what factors influenced them to have faith. Their answers were quite revealing:

1. Influence #1—Mother

2. Influence #2—Father

3. Influence #3—Pastor

4. Influence #4—Grandparent

5. Influence #5—Sunday School

6. Influence #6—Youth Group

7. Influence #7—Church Camp

8. Influence #8—Retreats[2]

D.   But the key finding was that Mom and Dad were two to three times more influential than any church program!

E.   How is religious life in the home today? Have the participants guess the answers to the following Search Institute survey of more than 11,000 participants from 561 congregations across 6 different denominations. Remember, these are the responses from churched teenagers!

1. What percentage of teenagers have a regular dialogue with their mother on faith/life issues? (12 percent)

2. What percentage of teens have a regular dialog with their father on faith/life issues? (5 percent)

3. What percentage of teenagers have experienced regular reading of the Bible and devotions in the home? (9 percent)

4. What percentage of youth have experienced a service-oriented event with a parent as an action of faith? (12 percent)[3]

F.   Share the following quote from George Barna: "We discovered that in a typical week, fewer than 10 percent of parents who regularly attend church with their kids read the Bible together, pray together (other than at meal times) or participate in an act of service as a family unit. Even fewer families—1 out of 20—have any type of worship experience together with their kids, other than while they are at church during the typical month."[4]

G. Discuss together the following questions:

1. Based on these statistical realities, how is religious life in the home today?

2. What do you think has caused this reality?

3. What has the church done or not done to cause or address this reality?

H. Let's hear what others are saying (share the following quotes):

1. "For all their specialized training, church professionals realize that if a child is not receiving basic Christian nurture in the home, even the best teachers and curriculum will have minimal impact. Once-a-week exposure simply cannot compete with daily experience where personal formation is concerned."[5]

2. "When a church—intentionally or not—assumes a family's responsibilities in the arena of spiritually nurturing children, it fosters an unhealthy dependence upon the church to relieve the family of its biblical responsibility."[6]

3. "Most certainly father and mother are apostles, bishops, and priests to their children, for it is they who make then acquainted with the gospel."[7]

4. "Most teenagers and their parents may not realize it, but a lot of research in the sociology of religion suggest that the most important social influence in shaping young people's religious lives is the religious life modeled and taught to them by their parents."[8]

5. And finally, my favorite quote from Dr. Roland Martinson of Luther Seminary: "What we ought to do is let the kids drop their parents off at church, train the parents and send them back into their mission field, their home, to grow Christians!"

I. Let's look at one other source: the Bible!

1. Have someone read the following passages:

   a. Deuteronomy 6:1-12

   b. Joshua 24:14-16

   c. Psalm 78

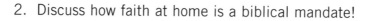

    2. Discuss how faith at home is a biblical mandate!

J.   Review: What have we discovered?

    1. Religious life in the home is more influential than the Church.

    2. Mom and Dad are two to three times more influential than any church program.

    3. *Yet* faith talk, devotions, Bible reading, prayer and service aren't happening in the home.

    4. Faith at home is biblically mandated and what God intended.

K.   Conclusion: Therefore, we need to get religious life, Christ and Christlike living back into the center of every home!

    1. One of the greatest existing challenges facing the Christian Church today is trying to figure out how we can equip the home to once again be the primary place where faith is nurtured through our existing ministry structures.

    2. State that this will be the focus of our next session.

L.   Take a 30-minute break.

IV.   Session II: Becoming a Valuable Partner (minimum 2 hours)

A.   Open with the following quote from George Barna: "The local church should be an intimate and valuable partner in the effort to raise the coming generation of Christ followers and church leaders, but it is the parents whom God will hold primarily accountable for the spiritual maturation of their children."[9]

B.   Discuss the following together:

    1. Is your church currently a valuable partner in bringing Christ and Christlike living into the home?

    2. Do unchurched people recognize your church as a valuable partner for them as parents or as a program center for their kids?

    3. Does your church have any of the following symptoms:

        a. An increasing number of parents who simply drop their children/youth off for the programs of the church but never attend themselves?

        b. A decreasing number of students attending or participating in the programs of the church as they get older?

        c. An increasing number of students and/or young adults who abandon their faith as they get older?

4. If your church has any or all of these symptoms, you're not alone. These are the symptoms of a church that has focused on having great programs and leaders who engage people at church but at the same time has gotten away from making the home—and Mom and Dad—the primary influencers of faith development.

5. Let's take a look at *how* we can equip the home once again to be the primary place where faith is nurtured *through* our existing ministry structures.

C. Go through the family ministry vision found in Section 1—Becoming a Church *of* Family Ministry.

1. Go through the add-a-silo versus church *of* family ministry models as explained on pages 14-15.

2. Discuss what it means to become a church *of* family ministry versus a church *with* family ministry.

3. Tell the audience that you are now going to focus the rest of your time together on *how* to become a church *of* family ministry.

D. The five keys for becoming a church *of* family ministry:

1. Key #1—make a long-term commitment

    a. In many ways, to become a church *of* family ministry requires a "back to the future" type of commitment. We're not going to change families overnight, but we do need to change families by reestablishing them and their homes as the primary place where faith is nurtured.

    b. George Barna describes it similarly: "Christian families taught the ways of God in their homes every day. Parents were expected to model a Spirit-led lifestyle for their children, and families were to make their home a sanctuary for God. In a very real sense, the home was the early church—supplemented by larger gatherings in the Temple and elsewhere, but never replaced by what took place in the homes of believers."[10]

2. Key #2—the commitment of the senior pastor

    a. Ask your senior pastor to share his/her passion and commitment for becoming a church *of* family ministry.

    b. How has God put this vision on your pastor's heart?

3. Key #3—a part of the mission/vision/strategy of the church

    a. Do your church's mission, vision and strategy accurately reflect your commitment to be a church *of* family ministry?

b. What changes could/should you make?

       c. How will these changes be shared with the congregation?

  4. Key #4—commit the resources necessary

       a. Does the church have the resources that will be needed to make this initiative happen?

       b. Are there any additional funds/resources that will be needed?

       c. How will those funds be secured?

  5. Key #5—involve all the ministries

       a. State how each ministry of the church, represented here today, has a role to play in the church becoming a church *of* family ministry.

       b. Go through and explain the Take It Home events from Section 3 and how these can serve as the backbone for your faith at home initiative as a congregation.

       c. Give each ministry 30 to 60 minutes to discuss what they could do to help make the faith at home movement happen. Questions they should discuss include:

          i. How can we contribute to becoming a church *of* family ministry?

          ii. How can we partner with our people to bring Christ and Christlike living back into the home?

          iii. What Take It Home event(s) could we initiate or help make happen?

          iv. Is there another ministry we should partner with to help make this happen?

       d. Bring everyone back together and list the ideas each ministry came up with on a whiteboard.

       e. Organize the ideas by establishing the dates and times for each Take It Home event.

       f. Determine who will provide the leadership for each event.

  E. Closing the session

    1. Conclude by stating that today was the beginning of a long-term work that God wants to do in and through you as a church.

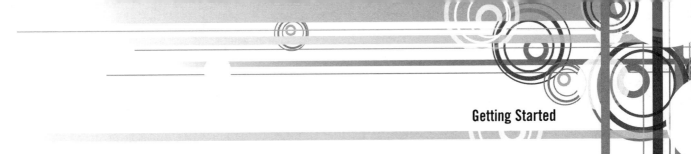

2. Celebrate the fact that you now have the beginning framework for your faith at home initiative that will influence and transform families for years to come!

3. Commit the decisions that were made to prayer.

4. Close by sharing the date for next year's summit, where you will evaluate and add more layers to your faith at home initiative.

Notes

1. Search Institute is a nonprofit, nonsectarian research and educational organization that advances the well-being and positive development of children and youth through applied research, evaluation, consultation, training, and the development of publications and practical resources for educators, youth-serving professionals, parents, community leaders and policy makers. Phone: 1-800-888-7828. Website: www.search-institute.org.

2. For the complete results, see Mark Holmen, *Faith Begins at Home* (Ventura, CA: Regal Books, 2006), p. 43.

3. *Effective Christian Education: A National Study of Protestant Congregations*, copyright 1990 by Search Institute SM. No other use is permitted without prior permission from Search Institute, 615 First Avenue NE, Minneapolis MN 55413.

4. George Barna, *Transforming Children into Spiritual Champions* (Ventura, CA: Regal Books, 2003), p. 78.

5. Marjorie Thompson, *Family, the Forming Center* (Nashville, TN: Upper Room Books, 1996).

6. Barna, *Transforming Children into Spiritual Champions*, p. 81.

7. Martin Luther, "The Estate of Marriage, 1522," quoted in Walther Brand, ed., *Luther's Works* (Philadelphia, PA: Fortress Press, 1962), p. 46.

8. Christian Smith, *Soul Searching* (New York: Oxford University Press, 2005), p. 56.

9. Barna, *Transforming Children into Spiritual Champions*, p. 83.

10. George Barna, *Revolution* (Carol Stream, Illinois: Tyndale House Publishers, 2005), p. 24

Section 3
Take It Home
Event Outlines

Baby Dedication or Infant Baptism

Target Age of Children

Newborns

Goal of Take It Home Event

To establish the partnership between parents and the church in passing on the faith to our children and children's children. Infant dedication or baptism, whichever your church observes, can either be simply a ritual we perform or it can be treated as the beginning of a lifelong partnership.

Preparing for the Event

- Depending on the size of your church, determine if you desire to meet individually with parents who wish to have their child dedicated or baptized or you may want to meet as a group. This material can work in either context.
- Send the Dedication or Infant Baptism Take It Home Event Letter (p. 56) 7 to 10 days in advance of your meeting or class to prepare people for this Take It Home Event. Customize the letter to fit the type of service your church performs for young children.
- Make copies (at least two per family) of the Will You Be My Child's Godparent? letter (p. 57). Explain at the event the history and purpose of godparents and allow parents the choice of whether to ask someone to be the godparents of their child.
- Collect the following: Bible, a picture of your parents and/or grandparents.

Event Outline

Explain It

After everyone has arrived, begin by showing a picture of your parents and/or grandparents. Ask the group to guess who you most look like. Then share who you most act like.

Ask others to share their pictures and who they look and act like. If you have a large group, let them share in smaller groups.

Ask parents to talk among their group about who, at this early age, their babies most look like.

Mention that even at this early age, we are already passing things on to our children.

Ask, "What is one thing you hope to pass on to your child?" "What do you not want to pass on to your child?"

Explain that in the book of Deuteronomy God gave some very specific instructions in raising children. The word "Deuteronomy" means "repetition of the law." Throughout Deuteronomy Moses is "repeating" the basic will and commands of God to the Israelites. If you were to read the entire book it would sound like a broken record.

Ask, "Why did Moses record this information in this way?"

Answer #1—Deuteronomy 6:2: "So that you, your children and their children after them may fear the LORD your God as long as you live by keeping all his decrees and commands that I give you."

Moses' intent was that God's people would know what is right and wrong and live with a proper respect, sometimes driven out of fear, for what is right and wrong.

Ask parents to think about this question: "How did your parents teach you right from wrong?"

Answer #2—Deuteronomy 6:2: "So that you may enjoy long life."

God wants us, and our families to enjoy long life! He wants us to enjoy life here and enjoy life beyond that which we will have here on earth.

Ask, "Is there anything more you could want for you and your child? What does the Bible say that will allow us to enjoy long life?"

- Deuteronomy 6:4-7—Love the Lord
- Deuteronomy 6:10-12—Don't forget the Lord.
- Deuteronomy 6:13-19—Follow and serve the Lord, not other gods.
- Deuteronomy 6:20-25—Obey the Lord

What does the Bible say is the key to making this happen in your home? In Deuteronomy 6:6 it says this commitment has to be on YOUR HEART!

If you want your child to love the Lord, follow the Lord, make godly decisions and obey the Lord, then YOU need to love the Lord, follow the Lord and obey the Lord!

Deuteronomy 6:7 says that faith needs to be lived out at home! It doesn't say, "Bring your kids to church and let the church impress it on their hearts." That doesn't work. Faith is caught as much as it's taught.

The Significant Religious Influences Survey[1] states that over 250,000 Christian teens who had a strong faith were asked what were the things that influenced them to have the life impacting faith they have. The answers were quite revealing:

- Number 1 reason why kids have faith? Mom
- Number 2 reason why kids have faith? Dad

Mom and dad are two to three times more influential than any church program! What, then, is the role of the church?

- To equip you, the parents, to pass on the faith to their children and,
- To reestablish the home as the primary place where faith is nurtured and,
- To be a lifelong partner for you and your family.

Thanks for the opportunity to partner with you!

Inspire Them

As you can see, dedication/baptism is just the beginning of a journey we are going to take together with you, your child and even your child's child. Here's something you can do now that can help you on this long-term journey.

A tradition that has existed for centuries, yet is on the decline in America, is making yourself available to godly people, called godparents. Here are some of the characteristics of godparents:

- People who have gone before you and lived a godly life, especially in the way they raised their children to know and follow Jesus;
- Lifelong spiritual mentors for you and your family to whom you would feel comfortable turning to for advice and support;
- Accountability partners holding you true to your commitment to love, follow, and obey the ways of God;
- Another spiritual voice and example in the life of your child.

You were asked to think of two people or couples who, in your perspective, did a good job raising their children to know and follow Jesus. Ask, "Have you considered inviting them to be at the dedication or baptism and fulfill the role of godparents?" In preparation for your child's dedication or baptism we would like to encourage you to identify and ask two people or couples to serve as your child's godparents and attend the service if at all possible. Distribute and read through the letter, "Will You

Be My Child's Godparent?" Have several extras available for parents to give to prospective godparents.

Model It

Some churches offer a baby dedication or baptism service a couple of times a year and include many babies at one time. Other churches have services throughout the year as requested by the families. At this time, go through specific instructions for the dedication or baptism service your church performs. Explain that this service is a public declaration and commitment for families and the church. A proposed format for a dedication/baptism service, with a great FaithChest® gift idea, has been provided on page 58, if you choose to use it.

Practice It

Provide all the details for the date and time of the dedication or baptism so that families can invite extended family and friends.

Take It Home

Prepare a special gift for families after the dedication or baptism service. Some churches provide certificates and baby Bibles. Other churches give handmade baby quilts or keepsake photo albums, or a FaithChest® (see the sample service for more information).

Suggested Resources

Holmen, Mark. *Faith Begins at Home.* Ventura, CA: Regal Books, 2005.

I Love to Look! Bible Story Pictures. Ventura, CA: Gospel Light, 1997.

Find additional resources at www.faithbeginsathome.com.

Ongoing Tradition Idea

Send a card or gift on the one-year anniversary of the dedication or baptism. At one church I served, the women's ministry decided to personally deliver a gift on the one-year anniversary of each child's dedication/baptism. The women's ministry director asked for a list of all the dedications/baptisms that were done the previous year. She was provided a list of the names of the children along with the parent names and household addresses. She then assigned two women to personally deliver a gift on the one-year anniversary date of the child's dedication/baptism. The gift was a nighttime devotional CD that the parents could play as their child would go to sleep at night. The family also received a card with the gift that read, "Happy Dedication/Baptism Anniversary! Thank you for the opportunity to partner with you to pass on the faith to (name of child). May the Lord continue to bless you and your family."

Note

1. Search Institute is a nonprofit, nonsectarian research and educational organization that advances the well being and positive development of children and youth through applied research, evaluation, consultation, training and the development of publications and practical resources for educators, youth-serving professionals, parents, community leaders and policy makers. Phone: 1-800-888-7828. Website: www.search-institute.org.

Date

Dear (name)

Greetings in the name of Christ!

We are so excited that you have come to (name of your church) seeking to have your child dedicated or baptized. This is a significant first step in you and your child's faith journey and I can't wait to meet with you on (date) at (time) in (location).

To help prepare for our time together, I would appreciate if you would do the following:

- Bring your child! This event is all about (name of child) so be sure to bring him or her along. I can't wait to meet him or her!
- Bring pictures of your parents and if possible, grandparents. If you adopted your child, bring pictures of his or her biological parents if possible.
- Read Deuteronomy 6. We will be discussing it when we get together.
- Bring the names of two Christian individuals and or couples who, from your perspective, have done a good job of raising their children to know Jesus.

Thank you again for the opportunity to (dedicate or baptize) your child. I am looking forward to getting together with you.

In Christ's Service,

Congratulations! You are being asked to be a godparent and this is a huge honor. You have displayed, through the way you have lived your life and passed on the faith to your children, that God is in the center of your life and your family.

Another family is desiring to do the same thing with their newborn child and they are making the commitment to be an "as for me and my household we will serve the Lord" family (see Joshua 24:15) by having their child dedicated/baptized at (name of church) on (date).

You are receiving this letter because they are desiring to surround themselves, and their child, with a few spiritual mentors who will encourage, support and hold them accountable to this commitment.

The tradition of godparenting has existed for centuries, yet is seemingly on the decline in America due to the fact that many people do not understand the role and responsibilities that go with being a godparent. Here is what is being asked of you as a godparent.

- The Role of Godparents—Godparents are meant to be people who have done their best to live a godly life, learning from their mistakes and raising their children to know, love and follow Jesus. Godparents will serve as lifelong spiritual mentors who will be openly available to be sought out for advice and support. Godparents also serve as accountability partners holding the parents and godchild true to their commitment to love, follow and obey the ways of Christ. And finally, godparents serve as another spiritual voice and example in the life of the child.
- The Responsibilities of Godparents—Godparents should pray for their godchild and family daily. The godparent should also play an active role in helping pass on the faith to the godchild through regular and repeated interaction with him or her. One suggestion is that the godparent sends a card and faith building gift to his or her godchild on the anniversary of the dedication/baptism date every year. Everyone else will remember the child's birthday; it's your responsibility to make sure your godchild remembers his or her dedication or baptism birthday! And finally, if at all possible, the godparent should attend the dedication/baptism service standing with the family and making the same commitment with them to help raise this child to know the love and saving grace of God!

Being asked to be a godparent is a great thing! May the Lord bless you as you consider this wonderful opportunity.

Begin by introducing the family, other children and their godparents to the congregation.

Affirmation Questions

Question to the Family—Do you desire to be an "As for me and my household, we will serve the Lord" family? If so please say, "We do!"

Question to the Parents—As we discussed when we met together, you, the parents, are the biggest influence in the faith development of your child. In Joshua 24 it says, "As for me" before it says "and my household." In Deuteronomy 6 it says, "These commandments that I give you are to be upon YOUR HEARTS" before it says "Impress them on your children." The Bible is clear: you the parents are the ones with the primary responsibility for passing on the faith to this precious child that God has blessed you with. Therefore I ask you, as parents, will you love, serve and obey the Lord will all your heart, soul and strength, setting the example your child needs in speech and in life, training your child in the way they should go so when he/she is older he/she will not turn from it? If so, please say "We will with the help of God."

Question to the Godparents—You have been asked by this family to serve as a godparent to (child's name) because of the way you have lived your life for God and raised your children to know and love the Lord. Will you accept the role of godparent and pray for this child and family daily? Will you also serve as a lifelong spiritual mentor and accountability partner holding the parents and godchild true to their commitment to love, follow, and obey the ways of Christ? If so please reply, "By the grace of God I/we will."

Question to the Congregation—We are called the family of God and therefore we are extended members of this family and they need us as well. Therefore I ask you as a body, will you encourage, support and sustain this family as they raise this child to know the love of Jesus Christ? If so, please reply, "We will!"

Perform the Dedication/Baptism

Baptize or dedicate your child according to your tradition.

Presentation of a FaithChest®

A FaithChest® is a small, hope chest that has been made by the members of the congregation. For plans and permissions to make a FaithChest® go to the Youth and Family Institute website at www.youthandfamilyinstitute.org. You can download kit plans to build a chest or purchase a kit. Different groups in the church may contribute items for the chest. It might include a certificate, Bible, and other meaningful items.

This FaithChest® is a symbol of our intention to work together with you the parents and you the godparents to provide resources that will help you pass on the faith to (name of child.) One day, this faith chest will be filled with resources that helped your child know the love of Jesus Christ and when your child has a child of his or her own (as hard as that is to believe now but it will go by so quickly!) you will be able to give your child this FaithChest® that he or she can use to pass on the faith to his or her child.

Closing Prayer and Family Blessing

May the Lord continue to bless you and keep you. May the Lord continue to make His face shine on you and be gracious to you. May the Lord continue to look upon you with favor and give you peace. In the name of the Father, and the Son and Holy Spirit. Amen.

Family Blessings

Target Age of Children

Two-year-olds

Goal of Take It Home Event

To establish the ritual of praying God's blessing over your child on a daily basis.

Preparing for the Event

- Duplicate Bible Blessings and Family Blessings handouts (pp. 64-65), one per family.
- On quality paper, duplicate copies of the blessings on pages 66-70. Prepare a variety so that families may choose their favorite blessing.
- Collect a Bible for each family and have a whiteboard and markers available.

Event Outline

Explain It

Ask the group to think of ways that you can bless people (things you say when people sneeze, things you say when someone is hurting or in need). How do people curse others? (Put-downs. Cursing. Negative comments.)

Ask, "Which do you hear most often? Which are most people better at?" Ask whether the parents experienced being blessed or cursed on a regular basis in the home.

Ask a volunteer to read aloud Numbers 6:22-27, from the Bible Blessings handout.

Ask, "What is the key to blessing?" The Lord. It is about Him and tapping into His power and authority.

Ask, "Why do we bless?"

Reason 1: "So they will put my name on the Israelites." Whose name do you want on your child? Nike? Reebok? Yankees? Cubs? Do you want your child to be known as God's child? Other names last only a season; God's name is eternal.

Reason 2: "And I will bless them." What does God's blessing look like? Read or have a parent read Deuteronomy 28:1-14 aloud. Write a brief version of the blessings on the whiteboard as you come to them. Ask, "Which of these blessings appeals to you the most? What might happen if your child received these blessings?"

Inspire Them

Read the following story as told by Mark Holmen or find someone in your church who has established the ritual of family blessings in the home and have him or her share a testimony.

"When my daughter was between two and three years old we attended a Family Blessing Take It Home Event at our church. Now before going any further, you need to realize that the idea of blessing your child was a completely foreign concept to both my wife and I. After receiving some biblical teaching about the significance of blessing your children the leaders then introduced to us a man by the name of Rolf Garborg and he began to speak. Rolf Garborg, author of *The Family Blessing*, shared with us that he started a ritual of saying a blessing over his daughter every evening. When his daughter was an infant he would go into her room every night and say a blessing over her. 'May the Lord continue to bless you and keep you. May the Lord continue to make his face shine on you and be gracious to you. May the Lord continue to look upon you with favor and give you peace. In the name of the Father, and the Son and the Holy Spirit. I love you. Amen.' As his daughter grew older, he continued the ritual all the way through the teenage years. He did admit that there was a period of time when she was a teenager that he would wait until she was asleep to give her the blessing but he continued the ritual all the same. His daughter continued to grow older as daughters do and it came time to send her to college. He and his wife dreaded the day that they would have to leave her at college, but they made a plan to unload her stuff, say their goodbyes in the dorm room and then they would grab each other's hands and head for the car with no looking back. The plan worked to perfection. The teary goodbyes had been said in the dorm room and Rolf and his wife were well on their way across the parking lot to the car when all of a sudden in the distance behind them they heard a familiar voice crying out, 'Mom, Dad, wait.' They had not planned for this contingency! They stopped in their tracks, turned around, and as their daughter came running up to them with tears in her eyes she said, 'You forgot to bless me.' And there in the parking lot they huddled together and said, 'May the Lord continue to bless you and keep you. May the Lord continue to make his face shine on you and be gracious to you. May the Lord continue to look upon you with favor and give you peace. In the name of the Father, Son and Holy Spirit. We love you. Amen.'

"When Rolf got done sharing that story, there wasn't a dry eye in the room. And guess what happened next? My wife and I raced home to see who could get to our daughter

first to begin the ritual of blessing her each evening! My wife won and every evening before my daughter goes to bed my wife will say, 'May the Lord bless you and keep you. May the Lord make his face shine on you and be gracious to you. May the Lord look upon you with favor and give you peace. In the name of the Father and the Son and Holy Spirit. I love you. Amen.'

"My daughter has been hearing this blessing every evening since she was two years old. When I was leaving for a trip to speak in Canada, I went into my now eleven-year-old daughter's room at 4:00 a.m. to give her a kiss goodbye. I didn't think she would wake up, but to my surprise she did. And when she saw me, she reached out her arm from underneath the covers and extended it to me and then in her groggy, half awake voice said the following words: 'Daddy, as you go on your trip may the Lord bless you and keep you. May He make His face shine on you and be gracious to you. May the Lord look upon you with favor and keep you safe. I love you, Daddy! Amen.'

"In Genesis 12:2 the Lord says, 'I will bless those who bless you.' The Lord has truly blessed me with an incredible daughter that we have prayed God's blessing over since she was two. I take none of the credit for how she has turned out as she is a way better kid than

I ever was. Yet every day I thank the Lord for the way He is blessing her and that's why every day my wife and I will continue to pray the Lord's blessing over her. May the Lord bless you as you bless your children in His name."

Model It

Choose one of the blessings from the Family Blessings handout. Ask parent volunteers to demonstrate for the group saying a blessing over their child. They can hold hands together or place their hands on the child's head.

Practice It

Distribute the Family Blessings handout and give families a minute to look over the blessings. Ask them to select a blessing and practice saying it over their child. Encourage them to use a variety of blessings.

Take It Home

Offer a variety of blessings (pp. 66-70) printed out on quality paper, suitable for an 8x10-inch (20.5x25.5 cm) frame. Allow families to choose one to take home. Encourage them to frame the blessing and hang it in their home where they will see it often.

Suggested Resources

Hayford, Jack. *Blessing Your Children* (book and video). Ventura, CA: Gospel Light, 2002.

Garborg, Rolf. *The Family Blessing*. For more information, contact Rolf Garborg, 4090-145th Street, Prior Lake, Minnesota, 55372. Phone: 612-440-7780.

Find additional resources at www.faithbeginsathome.com.

Numbers 6:22-27

The LORD said to Moses, "Tell Aaron and his sons, 'This is how you are to bless the Israelites. Say to them:

""'"The LORD bless you
and keep you;

the LORD make his face shine upon you
and be gracious to you;

the LORD turn his face toward you
and give you peace."'

"So they will put my name on the Israelites, and I will bless them."

Deuteronomy 28:1-14

"If you fully obey the LORD your God and carefully follow all his commands I give you today, the LORD your God will set you high above all the nations on earth. All these blessings will come upon you and accompany you if you obey the LORD your God: You will be blessed in the city and blessed in the country. The fruit of your womb will be blessed, and the crops of your land and the young of your livestock—the calves of your herds and the lambs of your flocks. Your basket and your kneading trough will be blessed. You will be blessed when you come in and blessed when you go out. The LORD will grant that the enemies who rise up against you will be defeated before you. They will come at you from one direction but flee from you in seven. The LORD will send a blessing on your barns and on everything you put your hand to. The LORD your God will bless you in the land he is giving you. The LORD will establish you as his holy people, as he promised you on oath, if you keep the commands of the LORD your God and walk in his ways. Then all the peoples on earth will see that you are called by the name of the LORD, and they will fear you. The LORD will grant you abundant prosperity—in the fruit of your womb, the young of your livestock and the crops of your ground—in the land he swore to your forefathers to give you. The LORD will open the heavens, the storehouse of his bounty, to send rain on your land in season and to bless all the work of your hands. You will lend to many nations but will borrow from none. The LORD will make you the head, not the tail. If you pay attention to the commands of the LORD your God that I give you this day and carefully follow them, you will always be at the top, never at the bottom. Do not turn aside from any of the commands I give you today, to the right or to the left, following other gods and serving them."

- To praise, petition for divine favor, wish someone will, convey favor
- To extend the hand and bring a touch of favor upon a person

Bless Your Children with God's Words

Ephesians 3:17-19

"And I pray that you, being rooted and established in love, may have power, together with all the saints, to grasp how wide and long and high and deep is the love of Christ, and to know this love that surpasses knowledge—that you may be filled to the measure of all the fullness of God."

Numbers 6:24-26

"The LORD bless you and keep you; the LORD make his face shine upon you and be gracious to you; the LORD turn his face toward you and give you peace."

Matthew 5:14,16

"You are the light of the world. A city on a hill cannot be hidden. In the same way, let your light shine before men, that they may see your good deeds and praise your Father in heaven."

Galatians 2:20

"I have been crucified with Christ and I no longer live, but Christ lives in me. The life I live in the body, I live by faith in the Son of God, who loved me and gave himself for me."

2 Thessalonians 2:16-17

"May our Lord Jesus Christ himself and God our Father, who loved us and by his grace gave us eternal encouragement and good hope, encourage your hearts and strengthen you in every good deed and word."

Ephesians 3:17-19

"And I pray that you, being rooted and established in love, may have power, together with all the saints, to grasp how wide and long and high and deep is the love of Christ, and to know this love that surpasses knowledge—that you may be filled to the measure of all the fullness of God."

Numbers 6:24-26

"The LORD bless you and keep you; the LORD make his face shine upon you and be gracious to you; the LORD turn his face toward you and give you peace."

Matthew 5:14,16

"You are the light of the world. A city on a hill cannot be hidden. In the same way, let your light shine before men, that they may see your good deeds and praise your Father in heaven."

Galatians 2:20

"I have been crucified with Christ and I no longer live, but Christ lives in me. The life I live in the body, I live by faith in the Son of God, who loved me and gave himself for me."

2 Thessalonians 2:16-17

"May our Lord Jesus Christ himself and God our Father, who loved us and by his grace gave us eternal encouragement and good hope, encourage your hearts and strengthen you in every good deed and word."

Family Devotions

Target Age of Children

Three-year-olds

Goal of Take It Home Event

To empower families to have a consistent, effective, successful, positive devotional experience together, thus forming a lasting discipline that will be a part of the child's life rhythm, continuing on for years and generations to come.

Note: My experience is that in most churches you are going to be speaking with two types of families. First, there are the long-time church families. Many of them have thought about or even tried to have a devotional time together at some point. Unfortunately, for various reasons, their attempts failed and their dreams never got off the ground. Some of these people feel guilty about their inability to follow through. Others may have a cynical attitude: "It just won't work with MY kids!" or "Have you seen our schedules lately?" Your goal is to ignite the fire of possibility in their hearts. You want to inspire and help them to believe again not only that it is worth the effort but that they can be successful.

The second group is new Christians who are experiencing church for the first time—or at least as adults. These people will tend to have more of an attitude of, "Show me how to do this and I'll do it." Many in this group are young couples who may have gone to church as children, dropped out in their late teens and twenties, and are now back to raise their kids in the church. This group has less of an idea about what "faith in the home" looks like, but will be more willing to try to develop it in their family. What this group needs is instruction on how to do what you are asking them to do. Simple, practical, and sometimes even basic, instruction will be needed. Devotions might be a foreign concept for them, so explaining the value of instilling this habit into their children will go a long way.

Preparing for the Event

- Duplicate "Bubbles of Ideas" (p. 77) and place one on each table.
- Collect the items needed for "Inspire Them" and put them in a large bag.
- Give a parent a devotional resource and ask him or her to prepare a brief devotional to lead during the event. (See Model It on page 76.)
- Provide a devotional resource for each family to take home with them so they can get started right away. Make a copy of the Monthly Devotional Calendar (p. 78) for each family.
- Collect a Bible, provide crayons and blank sheets of paper at each table and have a whiteboard and markers available.

Event Outline

Explain It

As families arrive, instruct them to sit together at a table and draw pictures of people and things they spend their time on (see sketches). Let them know they can get suggestions from the "Bubbles of Ideas" (p. 77).

After families have completed their pictures, let them share what they drew with the group. Ask for parents to share what they think the words "devotion" and "devoted" mean. Write their ideas on the whiteboard. After a few minutes, add additional thoughts: profound dedication; earnest attachment; undying loyalty; total faithfulness; constant commitment; unfailing allegiance; fervent determination; unwavering resolve.

Make these points as you explain the value of having family devotions.

- We all have things that we are devoted to. One way to discover those is by looking at where we spend our time.
- The more devoted we become, the more time we spend. (Share a personal example of something you are devoted to in your life.)

Parent   **Child**

- Ask, "Who do you think we are going to be more devoted—or committed—to when we talk about family devotions?" (God.)
- Family devotions involve carving out time as a family to spend time with God.
- The main point of starting devotions with very young children is building time with God into the rhythm of their lives at an early age. Much more important than the content of learning is simply the fact that you spend time regularly together focusing on God.
- Someday your children will grow up knowing their family was "profoundly dedicated, earnestly attached, undyingly loyal, totally faithful, constantly committed, unfailingly allegiant, fervently determined and had an unwavering resolve for God." Why? Not because you told them you were from time to time, or dragged them to church every week. It will be because you showed them your devotion every day you carved out time for your family to spend with God.

Inspire Them

Have a "Bag O' Success" with a variety of items in it. Each item should represent a tip for a successful devotional time. Invite a child to come up, pull out one of the items and identify it. Explain what the item represents and talk briefly about how it will help the family have a successful devotional time. Here are some ideas for "Bag O' Success" items and correlating tips to share with the families:

Item: Calendar
Tip: Be consistent.

Determine how many days a week you are going to commit to. Will you have devotions every day? Only on weekdays? Every other day? Do what works for your family.

Choose a natural time to implement devotions into your family routine. Ask families to share times that might work for them (e.g., first thing in the morning, at the breakfast table, after dinner, during bath time, before bedtime).

Keep at it for the long haul. Involve your kids in helping your family to stick with family devotions. Young children love to use stickers. (Optional: Distribute a calendar and a sheet or book of stickers to each family with instructions to add a sticker on the calendar for each day they successfully complete family devotions.)

Keep your family devotions calendar where your children can access and monitor it. Tell them that for every week of successful devotions your family will celebrate. Decide what kind of celebration will be meaningful to your family. Ask families to share what they might do to celebrate. Write these ideas on the board.

Item: Kitchen Timer
Tip: Keep it short.

Set the timer for about 45 to 60 seconds. Hold the timer up as you talk about this tip. When the timer goes off, it's time to move onto another tip.

A great principle to use with family devotions is: "Leave them wanting more." If you play a game until everyone is tired of it, you've played too long. If you end a game with the kids screaming, "Can't we just play one more round?" you will have them coming back eagerly to play next time. Finishing on a high-note creates anticipation for next time. The same principle applies to your devotional life at home. If at three minutes into the devotion your child is attentive, listening and engaged, but at four minutes they are ready to be done, then your devotion should be three minutes long. Keep it short. Less is more!

Item: Alphabet Blocks
Tip: Keep it simple.

Ask the children present at the event to sing their ABCs. Then say, "That was simple. That was successful."

One mistake in doing family devotions is making the material too complex for your child. The Bible and spirituality can be very abstract and hard for kids to understand. It can be challenging for adults. No one likes doing something they don't understand.

Write this equation on the whiteboard: Simple = Success

Let your families know that before they leave the session they will receive an age-appropriate resource to help

them be successful with simple devotions.

Item: Bubbles
Tip: Have fun.

Blow bubbles as you walk around the room and talk about this tip. Encourage the children to catch or pop the bubbles.

You don't hear this in church often enough: The number one goal of your devotion time is to have fun. Be silly, goofy and flexible. Enjoy this time with your family. Your children will learn that there is joy in their friendship with God. Family devotions should never become a drudgery.

Item: Ice Cream Container
Tip: Don't give up

This ice cream container stands for all or nothing. I can't just eat a little bit of ice cream. I either want a giant bowl or I'd rather just spare myself the guilt and eat none at all.

However, if you take this approach with your devotions you will fail. You will not be perfect in your devotional life. That's OK. Just because you've missed one, two or twelve days in a row, remind yourself to see every day as a new opportunity to get back on track.

You may even want to build some days off into your week. Maybe you commit as a family to having devotions five days a week with two optional days built in. Then, there is some margin for sickness, schedules or even laziness. This way you can also be an overachiever and get extra devotional credit if all seven days work out.

Whatever you do, don't let a bad patch stop you, don't be "all or nothing" when it comes to family devotions.

Have your parents and kids raise their right hands and repeat after you: "In the same way God forgives me I will forgive myself for missing days of devotions."

(Optional: If you really want to drive this point home, serve little cups of ice cream for everyone to eat as a statement of their commitment not to be all or nothing. You may choose to substitute cookies or candy for the ice cream if those options are easier in your setting.)

Item: Ping Pong Paddle
Tip: Involve the kids.

Ping Pong is played with two people who tap the ball back and forth to each other. Family devotions aren't a one-way street. They must engage parents and the kids.

Here are a couple of ways to "put the ball in your child's court." As you look at a devotional book, use the pictures to help you. Ask your children simple questions. For example, you may ask, "Is the girl in this picture happy or sad?" "Who loves us all the time no matter what?" "This little boy has a friend just like you. Who are your friends?"

Since children learn through repetition, take advantage of daily devotions that often have a short prayer or Bible verse at the beginning or end. Have your child repeat these after you read them in short phrases.

Did You Get the Tips?

If you want to go the extra mile, ask families to volunteer to role play the opposite of the tips that were shared. Meet with them briefly to explain what they should do. Encourage them to exaggerate their actions. Enjoy this segment and get silly with it. Ask the other families to suggest which tip would help the family be more successful with their devotions. Role-play ideas:

- **Be consistent:** Mom and dad are trying to remember the last time they had devotions. Both have different memories.
- **Keep it short:** The dad drones on and on and on. The mom keeps looking at her watch, sighing and shaking her head.
- **Keep it simple:** Have the dad read a complicated passage from a theology book as the child and mom are confused, shaking their heads and shrugging their shoulders.
- **Have fun:** The mom talks in a monotone voice, sighs a lot, and sounds tired and bored herself. Dad and the child look bored and are about to fall asleep.
- **Don't give up:** Child keeps asking when they can do family

devotions again. Mom and Dad keep responding with activities they have to do. Finally Mom and Dad say, "Maybe we just can't do devotions."

- **Involve the kids:** Mom and Dad do all the talking. The child sits separately, looking another direction.

Model It

Some people need to see what you are talking about. They hear all the tips, have the resource, and even listen to you describe the scenario, but seeing it drives the point home. Last year at our event a father and his three-year-old daughter did a devotion together for everyone to see. Not only was it great to experience a living example, but it was a wonderfully tender and heart-warming moment that was inspirational for everyone there.

Ask a family ahead of time to do a brief family devotion in front of your group. Give the parents the materials ahead of time to become familiar with them.

Practice It

Distribute a devotional resource to each family. Give the families a few moments to have a devotion together.

(Optional: If you are distributing a calendar with stickers [see Take It Home below], remind them to put a sticker on their calendars for today's date.)

Take It Home

Give each family a copy of the Monthly Devotional Calendar to take home, filling in the month and dates. Suggest each family use stickers or draw happy faces or other symbols on the days when they participate in family devotions together. Ask each family to set a realistic goal of how many days a week they plan to have devotions.

Suggested Resources

Barnhill, Carla and Elena Kucharik. *Blessings Every Day: 365 Simple Devotions for the Very Young.* Carol Stream, IL: Tyndale House Publishers, 2001.

FamilyTime Bible Storybook. Ventura, CA: Gospel Light, 2003.

Raising Up Spiritual Champions Newsletters. Ventura, CA: Gospel Light, 2007.

Find additional resources at www.faithbeginsathome.com.

How do you spend your time?

Monthly Devotional Calendar

MONTH: _____

SUNDAY	MONDAY	TUESDAY	WEDNESDAY	THURSDAY	FRIDAY	SATURDAY

My Church

Target Age of Children

Preschoolers or Four-Year-Olds

Goal of Take It Home Event

To allow families to have a memorable experience together at church as they learn how much they matter to the faith community.

Preparing for the Event

- Set out on each table a copy of Make a Paper Church (p. 84).
- Make one or more sample paper churches so families can see what they are going to make.
- Prepare activities for families to participate in during their treasure hunt around the church (see Model It for ideas and details) and refreshments to serve during discussion after the treasure hunt (see Practice It).
- Ask staff, board or elders to attend this event.
- Make a copy of the My Church mini booklet (pp. 85-88) for each family.
- Collect a Bible, scissors, glue, paper, tissue paper cut into small pieces, crayons; for each family—a 1x3-inch (2.5x7.5-cm) self-adhesive label and several small pictures of your church staff.

Event Outline

Explain It

As families arrive, instruct them to look at your paper church sample, follow the step-by-step instructions at their table, and work together to make a representation of your church. Encourage staff, board or elders to mingle with families as they work on their paper churches.

After families have worked for a while on their paper churches, encourage discussion with parents and their children with these questions:

- Parents, what do you remember about the church you grew up in?
- Kids, what is your favorite thing about our church?
- Who is someone you really like to see when you come to church?
- What is the church?

Ask the parents and their kids to do this finger play with you:

"Here is the church,

and here is the steeple.

Open the doors

and see all the people."

Discuss answers to these questions:

- How is the church a community of people?
- If the building you meet in were to burn down or get ruined in some way, would the church still exist?

A song I've sung for years expresses the wonderful truth about our church family: The church is people! It's not a location or a building. Everyone who loves and follows Jesus is the church together. Explain that the Bible describes the church as:

- a body, not a business (see Colossians 1:18,24; Romans 12:5);
- an organism, not an organization (see 1 Peter 2:5);
- a family, not an institution (see Galatians 6:10);
- a people, not a place (see 1 Peter 2:9).

Ask your families to look at the name of the church they put on their paper churches. See if they can figure out what might be added in the space below the name that might more accurately describe the church. After some responses, explain that "Meets Here" is missing from the sign out front. The sign should say that (Your Church's Name) Meets Here. Explain that the building is only the place you gather together in. The believers—people—make up the church.

Have the parents write the words "Meets Here" underneath the name of the church on their paper churches.

Ask, "Who is the most important person at church?" Allow some responses.

Read Romans 12:5 aloud: "Just as there are many parts to our bodies, so it is with Christ's body. We are all parts of it, and it takes every one of us to make it complete, for we each have different work to do. So we belong to each other, and each needs all the others" (*TLB*). Name some people in your church that most of the children would know, and explain what work they do for others in the church.

Ask the children whether they think they are an important part of your church. What do they do that is important to other believers? Tell them how everyone is important in the church community. Read the passage in 1 Corinthians 12:12-27. Ask volunteers to represent each body part as you read the passage.

Ask, "If the church building isn't really the church, why do we care about it?" Allow some responses. Ask the children if their home is important to them and why. Relate the church to a home for a church family. Talk about how it is a safe place where we gather as a family and that we should respect the church but also feel comfortable here. Ask them to think of ways they can help to take care of the building. Explain that everybody has a part in taking care of the building.

Inspire Them

Share what you love about your church and how the people have made a differ-ence in your life. Talk about the impact that children and their families have in your life. Express how grateful you are that each person in the room is a part of your children's ministry and your church.

Model It

Explain to the families that they will go together on an exploration like a treasure hunt around your church building. Remind them that the people they encounter on their exploration are people in their church family.

Have families form groups so they get to know other families from your church. After they get into groups, allow them a moment to introduce themselves to each other if they aren't acquainted. Then give them a few minutes to share a little about themselves before they go exploring:

- Where they live;
- How long they have been going to your church;
- An activity or hobby they love to do as a family.

Use a map or provide clues to lead family groups to the different places you want them to visit around the church. Lead families to places they wouldn't normally go to but might be intrigued by. They may seem obscure to you, but the children will find the exploration exciting and it will help them feel at home in your building. This treasure hunt can last from 20 to 30 minutes depending on the time available. You may wish to give each family a sheet on which the leaders they meet sign their names. The family group writes on the sheet what each leader does at the church.

At each destination have church leaders stationed. Ask these leaders to be prepared to introduce themselves to the families and explain what they do as a part of the church family. They should also get the names of all the families that come to their destination. This event is a golden opportunity for your staff to get to know your young families.

Because some staff might be busy during this time you can record them on video welcoming the children and their families. Put a sign on the TV instructing each group to press play to hear a special message from Pastor(s) and then ask them to rewind the tape before leaving. Other staff could simply provide a tape recording if they are unable to be there.

At each location each family can also receive something to make the exploration more exciting. At each location, families could:

- Learn an interesting fact about your church such as the name of first pastor, the year your church began, the number of people who attend or are members, a fact about your church's denomination, a little-known fact about your pastor;
- Collect puzzle pieces that will ultimately create a picture of the

church building. The picture could say, "Where my church family gathers!" To make these puzzles, take a picture of your church to a local print shop or search the Internet for "photo puzzles";

- Receive treats such as small pieces of candy;
- Collect index cards with a word or phrase from a Bible verse to put together (e.g., Ephesians 4:11-13);
- Collect Bible verses about the Church (e.g., Ephesians 4:3-6);
- Families could also engage in a challenge at each location (look up a Bible verse and recite it together, tell the leader one thing about themselves, make a shot in a hoop before leaving, etc.).

Practice It

After the treasure hunt, gather your families to talk about the experience over cookies or donuts and milk. If families received puzzle pieces or words from a Bible verse, give them time to put them together.

Ask families to share what their favorite part of the exploration was. What kinds of things did they learn that they didn't know before? Did they see any part of the building for the first time?

See how much people remembered with questions like these:

- Who remembers what Pastor (John's) favorite food is?

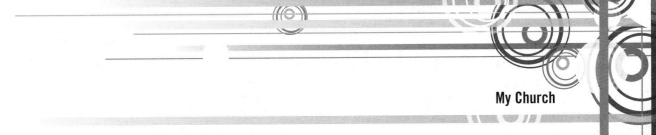

- Who remembers the Bible verse you looked up in (Mary's) office?
- Who remembers the color of the (banner in the sanctuary)?

Take It Home

Provide each family with a My Church mini-book (pp. 85-88) to complete together at home during the next week.

1. Color the church with your child to match the colors of your church.

2. Help your child cut out the church on the black lines and fold it on the dotted lines.

3. With your child, glue small pieces of tissue paper on the paper cross. Cut out the cross. Attach the cross to the church.

4. Attach the adhesive label to the front of the church and write your church name across the top. Leave an open space below the name.

5. Open the church and glue one or more pictures of the church staff on the inside. Ask your child who these people are. Write each person's name below the picture.

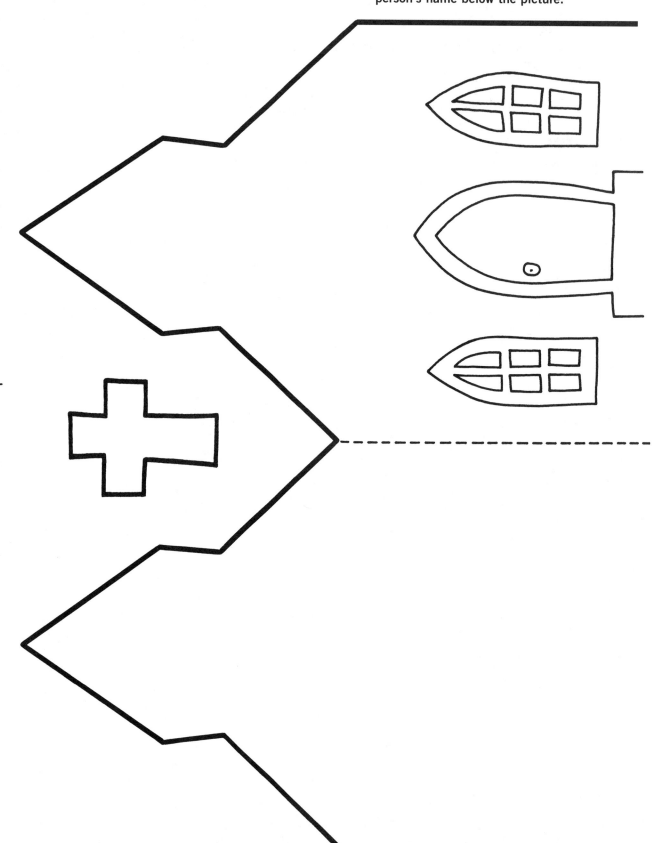

Make a Paper Church

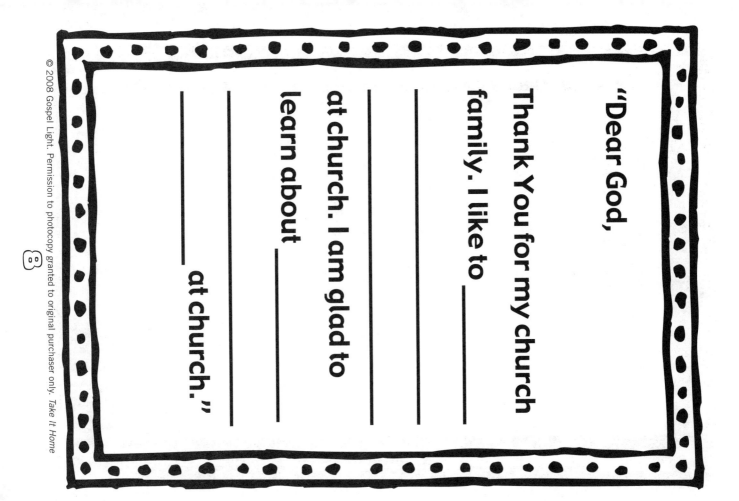

"Dear God,

Thank You for my church family. I like to _____

_____ at church. I am glad to

learn about _____

_____ at church."

8

MY CHURCH

1

"Keep on praying."
Ephesians 6:18

My Prayer List for My Church

"Dear friends, let us love
one another, for love
comes from God."
1 John 4:7

People at my church show love
for others when . . . .

Here are my friends at church:

6

3

"Let us do good to all people,
especially to those who belong
to the family of believers."
Galatians 6:10

I can help at my church by . . .

Here's a picture of me at my church:

Family Prayer

Target Age of Children

Kindergartners or Five-Year-Olds

Goal of Take It Home Event

To empower your families to develop the regular habit of prayer and thus connect the next generation to God in a powerful way.

Preparing for the Event

- Prepare shoe boxes (one per family) by covering them with white paper. Cut a slit in the box lid large enough for an index card to slip through. You will also need crayons or markers, scissors, stickers and index cards.
- Duplicate Prayer Bookmarks (p. 95) for each person attending the event.
- Set up three Learning Style Prayer Centers as instructed in Practice It (pp. 93-94).
- Make a copy of Prayers from the Psalms for Your Family (p. 96) for each family.
- Collect a Bible for each family and have a whiteboard and markers available.

Event Outline

Explain It

As families arrive, give each one a pre-pared shoe box and a Prayer Bookmark page. For shoe boxes, instruct them to make Prayer Boxes by coloring the boxes and decorating them with stickers. Encourage parents to work with their children to think of and write down on index cards the names of people and things they are praying for and drop them in the box.

For Prayer Bookmarks, instruct families to cut out the bookmarks, color in the letters and add other decorations as desired.

After families have worked for a while on their Prayer Boxes and Bookmarks, call them together and tell them that that the purpose of this event is to empower families to develop the regular habit of prayer.

Briefly make these statements:

- Prayer connects children to God in a powerful way;
- Plan to learn about prayer along with your children;
- Don't expect to be prayer experts. You don't have to be wonderfully eloquent, using big theological adjectives as you pray;
- Just take the initiative to pray, be authentic and let God do the rest.

Ask families to think of an answer together to this question: What is prayer? Give them several minutes to discuss it and then ask families to share their answers. Write their ideas on the board. Here are some responses you might hear:

- Time with God;
- Communicating with God;
- Talking to God;
- Asking God for help;
- Listening to God;
- Letting God lead your life;
- Telling God how much you love Him;
- Asking God to help others.

Ask, "Why is prayer important?" Let families share their answers. Here are some possible responses:

- Helps us know God;
- Reminds us that God is with us;
- Reminds us God can help us;
- Helps us share our burdens or hard times with God.

Remind parents that these are fundamental things we want their children to be confident in. Ask, "Why don't we pray?" Let families share some of their ideas and ask parents to read the Scripture passages included below.

- Intimidated—Sometimes we feel like when we pray, we must talk for a long time or use big words, but Jesus tells us this isn't true. Have a parent read Matthew 6:7-8: "When you pray, don't talk on and on as people do who don't know God. They think God likes to hear long prayers. Don't be like them. Your Father knows what you need before you ask" (*CEV*).

- Not a habit—Praying regularly may be something we are not used to doing.
- Busy—Our lives may be over-scheduled so that we feel we have no time for prayer. Have a parent read Mark 4:19: "But the worries of this life, the deceitfulness of wealth and the desires for other things come in and choke the word, making it unfruitful."
- Not effective—Can God hear us when we talk to him? Have a parent read Psalm 4:3: "The LORD will hear when I call to him."

Two Approaches

Encourage your parents to develop a life of prayer in two different ways. First, establish a routine prayer time. All of us need routine. Routine is what helps us remember things that are important and stay consistent. We must establish a time when we take a moment to talk to God every day.

Ask the families to share different times that might work for them to pray together every day:

- Before bed;
- Before meals;
- Morning;
- Before school;
- Mom or Dad gets home from work;
- Car ride to or from someplace you go as a family.

Secondly, look for prayer opportunities. Perhaps even more important than having an established prayer time is taking advantage of life opportunities to teach your kids not only about prayer, but also that God is our strength and source of power and encouragement in this life. When we turn to God throughout our day, we demonstrate for our kids in a very powerful way that He is with us 24/7 and is always available to us, His children.

Ask a parent to read 1 Thessalonians 5:17: "And never stop praying." What might some good prayer opportunities be?

- When someone is hurt. Instead of simply doing the traditional "Let mommy kiss it better," use a child's injury to teach them that we can talk to God when we are hurt. A simple prayer for comfort can be very significant.
- When someone is sad. Children may feel sad about various life events. Teach your kids to truly cast their burdens onto Jesus by praying to Him, honestly expressing their feelings.
- When someone is scared. Children may feel scared of the dark, going to school, clowns (they are scary when you think about it!), or the neighbor's dog. Encourage your child to tell God about his or her fears and ask for His courage and protection.
- When someone is successful. Celebrate your child's success by praising God for the abilities and gifts He has given them.
- When you're trying something new. As your children grow, they will inevitably try new sports, new skills and new hobbies. Remind

them to ask God for help and wisdom as they grow and learn.

Inspire Them

Share the following story by Dave Teixeira or one of your own that makes the point about prayer on the go.

"My wife is an animal lover and more specifically a dog lover. As a result she is very sensitive about how people take care of their animals. She gets very nervous when people let their dogs ride freely in the beds of their trucks. So, in our car, every time we spot a dog riding down the road in the bed of a truck a prayer is sent up for that pooch. This habit has rubbed off on my daughter, now three years old, who literally freaks out and demands we instantly pray every time she spots a dog in a truck-bed. Excessive use of prayer? Perhaps, but the wonderful part about this story is that prayer has broken out of the prayers routinely expressed in church and before meals and into our car on any given day at any given moment. We also take advantage of prayer opportunities when we see car accidents or ambulances as we're driving on the road. The point is to look for opportunities to speak out in prayer at a moment's notice throughout the day."

Model It

What do we say when we pray? Teach families to pray in four main areas. Use the ACTS acronym as a memory tool for this strategy:

- Adoration
- Confession
- Thanksgiving
- Supplication

A more kid-friendly version is PAST:

- Praise (Adoration)
- Apologize (Confession)
- Supplication (Ask)
- Thank (Thanksgiving)

Lead families in a brief prayer time based on the PAST acronym. First, we PRAISE God for who he is. Read these verses aloud: Psalm 48:1—"How great is the LORD, how deserving of praise" (*NLT*); Psalm 150:6—"Let everything that has breath praise the LORD."

Then ask families to share some things about God that we can praise Him for. If they need help to get started, ask them to complete this sentence with a word: I praise God because He is (loving, awesome, powerful, merciful, all-knowing, smart, faithful).

As the families share, write the words up on the whiteboard. After the sharing ends, ask everyone to join you in praising God. Pray, "God, we praise You because You are (read all the words families have shared). In Jesus' name, amen!"

Next, we APOLOGIZE to God for things we've done wrong. Billy Graham said, "The Christian life is not a constant high. I have my moments of deep discouragement. I have to go to God in prayer with tears in my eyes, and say, 'O God, forgive me,' or 'Help me.'"[1] Read 1 John 1:9 aloud: "But if we confess our sins to God, he can always be trusted to forgive us and take our sins away" (*CEV*).

Ask families to share some things they could apologize to God for. If they need help to get started, ask them to complete this sentence with a word: God, I'm sorry that I (didn't clean my room, was impatient with a family member, was mean to my Mom, told a lie).

As the families share, write the apologies on the whiteboard. After the sharing ends, ask everyone to join you in saying sorry to God. Pray, "God, we are sorry for all the things we have done wrong. We are sorry for the times we (read all the phrases families have shared). In Jesus' name, amen!"

Third, God also wants us to ASK for things we and other people need! Read Matthew 7:7-8 aloud: "Ask and it will be given to you; seek and you will find; knock and the door will be opened to you. For everyone who asks receives; he who seeks finds; and to him who knocks, the door will be opened."

Ask families to share some things they could ask God for. If they need help getting started, ask them to complete this sentence: "God, could you please (be with Grandma this week, help me with my spelling test next Wednesday, direct a bid decision I have coming up at work, help me get along with my brother)."

As the families share, write the requests on the whiteboard. After the sharing ends, ask everyone to join you in asking God for these things. Pray,

"God, we need You so much and we are so grateful that You would hear our requests. We ask that You (read all the phrases families have shared). In Jesus' name, amen!"

Finally, we can THANK God for answered prayers, things He has done in our lives and also for the blessings we and others have received. Read Psalm 107:1 aloud: "Give thanks to the LORD, for he is good; his love endures forever."

Ask families to share some things they could thank God for. If they need help getting started, ask them to complete this sentence: "God, thank You for (healing my dog, keeping Dad safe on his trip, making me feel better, always being with me, for giving me such great friends, giving us the Bible, our church)."

As the families share, write the things we are thankful for on the whiteboard. After the sharing, ask everyone to join you in thanking God for these things. Pray, "God, we thank You so much for all that You do. Thank You for (read all the phrases families have shared). In Jesus' name, amen!"

Practice It

Explain to parents that everyone learns and processes information in different ways. People tend to be visual, auditory or tactile. To help you as parents engage your children during prayer, we want to give you ideas for each of these three learning styles. For example, children who learn visually will love praying for people as you flip through a photo album and look at their pictures. Technically savvy families may create a slideshow on a computer with pictures of people to pray for scrolling across the screen.

If you have children who learn best in auditory ways, ask them to listen as you pray aloud and after the prayer discuss what you prayed for. You may also read prayers such as Matthew 6:9-13 or prayers in a devotional book aloud in unison, or alternating sentences.

Children who learn primarily through tactile methods will enjoy drawing pictures of things to pray about, or even collecting a pile of rocks and saying a prayer as each rock is dropped into a container. Another option for tactile learners is to offer up a prayer to God with each shot of a basketball into a hoop. Be creative as you look for tactile prayer ideas: play with clay as you pray, or make a Prayer Sandwich (bread slice = praise, peanut butter = apologize, jelly = ask and bread slice = thank). (Note: The clay does not necessarily have to create an image of what the child wants to pray about. Tactile kids usually just need something tactile going on to help them focus.)

Divide your families into three groups. Send each group to one of your three Learning Style Prayer Centers. If time permits, each group takes a turn at each center.

Visual Prayer Center

At this station have pictures of people and things to pray for (President, environment, school, church, brothers and sisters, grandparents, people who are sick, friends). As you hold up each picture, ask both children and parents to volunteer to pray!

Auditory Prayer Center

At this center, have everyone cup their hands over their mouths and explain that this is a whisper prayer and that they can pray anything they want as long as it is whispered into their hands. Instruct the families to whisper:

- God, I praise You that You are _____.
- God, I am sorry for _____.
- God, would You please _____.
- Thank You, God, for _____.

Tactile Prayer Center

At this center, provide a ball or bean bag. Each time a person tosses the ball or bean bag, he or she calls the name of someone to pray for or a request.

Take It Home

Send home a Prayers from the Psalms page with each family. Encourage them to read one of the prayers each day together and make it their own prayer or paraphrase it into their own words.

Suggested Resource

Vezey, Denis. *God Answers My Prayers.* Colorado Springs, CO: Chariot Victor Publishing, 1999.

Note

1. www.brainyquote.com (Accessed September, 2007).

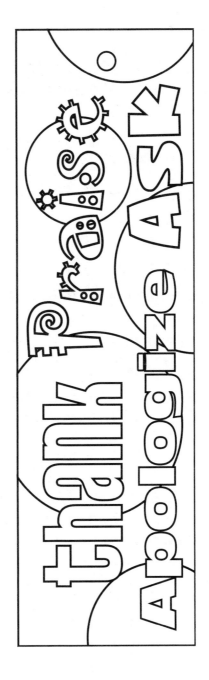

"Morning by morning, O Lord, you hear my voice; morning by morning I lay my requests before you and wait in expectation" (see Psalm 5:3).

"I will praise you, O Lord, with all my heart; I will tell of all your wonders" (Psalm 9:1).

"Forgive my hidden faults. Keep your servant also from willful sins; may they not rule over me" (see Psalm 19:12).

"Show me your ways, O Lord, teach me your paths; guide me in your truth and teach me, for you are God my Savior, and my hope is in you all day long" (Psalm 25:4-5).

"Have mercy on me, O God, according to your unfailing love; according to your great compassion blot out my transgressions. Wash away all my iniquity and cleanse me from my sin" (Psalm 51:1-2).

"May God be gracious to us and bless us and make his face shine upon us" (Psalm 67:1).

Family Service Projects

Target Age of Children

First Graders

Goal of Take It Home Event

To inspire and engage the family in being the hands and feet of Christ through church, community and global service as a family.

Preparing for the Event

- Ask a missionary family, Christian police officer, fireman or active member of the armed services to come to your event and share their experiences as a public servant (see p. 98). Ask them to keep the talk to 10 minutes or less and encourage them to tell as many stories as possible. Remind them to keep their testimony at a second grade level. Explain that the key point you want to communicate in the testimonies is that ordinary people are used by God to serve others and there is great joy in serving others. A sample invitation letter is provided on page 101.
- Make copies of the Encouragement Postcards (p. 102) so you have at least one per person. Provide postcard postage stamps as well.
- Place on individual cards or slips of paper the names and addresses of people in your congregation who are homebound, hospitalized or otherwise in need of a note of encouragement, at least one name and address per person.
- Make one Family Serve Booklet (pp. 103-104) per family, listing church, community and global service opportunities on the appropriate pages.
- Make 12 copies of the Family Serve Calendar (p. 105) for each family.
- Create a picture wall. If your church supports missionaries, display their pictures on the wall with a description of where each missionary serves. In addition, hang pictures of firemen, police officers, doctors, nurses, pastors, people in the armed forces. Display several pictures of Jesus.
- Cover each table with a paper tablecloth that can be written on. Collect a Bible and place a box of crayons and a few pens on each table. Have a whiteboard and markers available.

Event Outline

Explain It

As families arrive, ask them to sit around prepared tables. Direct the group's attention to the picture wall and ask, "What do you notice that the people pictured have in common?" After a few guesses, say that they are all pictures of people who serve us.

Ask for volunteers to pick out a picture and say how that person serves.

Ask them to think about the people who have served them personally in the past week. Families write the names of people on the paper that covers the table. Then invite volunteers to name some of the people who have served them.

Ask the children, "In what ways do your parents serve you?"

Ask the parents, "In what ways do your children serve you?"

Ask anyone to answer: "What are the characteristics of someone who serves?" Write the answers on the whiteboard.

Inspire Them

Introduce the person who will be sharing their testimony. "I would like you to hear from a person who serves God as a (name of occupation). Please join me in welcoming (name of the guest). Guest shares his or her testimony with group. Allow 8 to 10 minutes for sharing and approximately 5 minutes for questions.

Model It

Read the story below entitled "Jesus Is Coming" or ask volunteers to act it out as you read it.

A family sits together at home when the phone rings. The person calling identifies himself as Jesus and lets them know that He is going to be coming over that evening. After determining that the phone call was not a prank (due to the fact that the phone had been disconnected two days earlier!), the family realizes that they have to get things ready for Jesus' visit. They hastily begin cleaning up the house. The preparation involves replacing the pictures on the wall with crosses, hiding the variety of magazines on the coffee table and putting out the Bible. The teenage son discreetly removes some questionable items from under his bed. During this preparation and cleaning time the family has three separate visitors who come to the door. The first is someone asking for food donations for the local food bank, the second visitor is raising money for a battered women's shelter, and the final visitor has just been in a car accident and needs to use the phone to call for help.

On all three occasions the family pushes the visitor out the door exclaiming, "We are too busy right now preparing for a very important guest who is coming. Go next door." The family looks at the clock. It is one minute before midnight so they decide to really impress Jesus, as

He is sure to be coming any second. They sit down together, open the Bible randomly, and begin to read. The text they happen to turn to is Matthew 25:41-45.

"Then he will say to those on his left, 'Depart from me, you who are cursed, into the eternal fire prepared for the devil and his angels. For I was hungry and you gave me nothing to eat, I was thirsty and you gave me nothing to drink, I was a stranger and you did not invite me in, I needed clothes and you did not clothe me, I was sick and in prison and you did not look after me.' They also will answer, 'Lord, when did we see you hungry or thirsty or a stranger or needing clothes or sick or in prison, and did not help you?' He will reply, 'I tell you the truth, whatever you did not do for one of the least of these, you did not do for me.'"

By the time the family is done reading this text, the hour has struck midnight. The teenage son says, "I guess Jesus isn't coming after all." After a moment of silence the mother responds, "I think Jesus was already here."

Discussion Questions

Lead families in discussing the story. Ask the following questions:

- What did you learn from that story? What was the main point?
- Is serving others important to Jesus? Let's look at what the Bible says. Read Matthew 20:28 and Luke 22:27 aloud.
- What should our attitude be towards serving others? Read Ephesians 6:7, Galatians 5:13 and 1 Peter 4:10 aloud.
- Who are people who serve God today? Have families tell names of people who serve God.

Practice It

Explain to the group that now they will have an opportunity to share in a family service project activity. Begin the activity by explaining that in your congregation you have people who are homebound, hospitalized or hurting in some way. One of the ways we can serve them is to send them a card of encouragement.

On each table you will find Encouragement Postcards as well as the names and addresses of people in our congregation who are homebound, hospitalized or otherwise in need of a note of encouragement.

Give families five minutes to color the cards and share an encouraging message like "We prayed for you today" or "Remember God is with you." Have the parents write the name and address on the card.

When the card is completed, ask each family to say a short prayer for the person who will be receiving the card.

Then ask the following questions:

- How difficult was that activity?
- How does that make you feel knowing that you have served to

encourage someone you don't even know?

- How do you think the person who receives your card might feel?

Take It Home

Read the following quote from Peter Benson's book, *All Kids Are Our Kids*.

"Service to others is valuable both to the community and to the young person who serves, but we have a long way to go in engaging youth consistently in serving others (with adults being even less likely to be active volunteers). According to our surveys of American youth, most middle school and high school students do not engage in regular service. When asked how much time they had spent helping others in the past week, 52 percent said they had spent no time. Another 22 percent said they had spent one hour, with 26 percent reporting spending two or more hours."[1]

Give each family a blank Family Serve Calendar. Explain that the calendar is blank because when they get home the children are to draw in the open space in the middle a picture for the month that best symbolizes the month for your family. The calendar does not have days or dates so that each family may select one act of service to do each month.

Give each family a Family Serve Booklet. Look at the booklet together. Explain that in the booklet families will see ways they can serve at church, in the community as well as globally!

Explain the different serving opportunities in each section. Invite volunteers to suggest other opportunities as well.

As a family, go through the Family Serve Booklet and select the 12 projects you would like to do during the next year. It's OK to repeat a service activity and do it more than one month. (Note: For page 3 of the booklet, consider physical labor such as roadside cleanup, as well as people-oriented community service such as mentoring, visiting people in a nursing home, etc. For page 4, list opportunities for families to participate in programs that serve people of other nations.)

At home, once all 12 monthly pictures have been drawn and all 12 acts of service have been determined, hang the calendar in a prominent place in your home. When people ask why you have a calendar with no days or dates explain that you are a "As for me and my household we will serve the Lord" family!

Suggested Resources

Jenny Lynn Friedman. *The Busy Family's Guide to Volunteering*. Robins Lane Press, 2003.

The Big Book of Service Projects. Ventura, CA: Gospel Light, 2001.

Daphne Rose Kingma and Dawna Markova. *Random Acts of Kindness*. San Francisco, CA: Conari Press, 2002.

Find additional resources at www.faithbeginsathome.com.

Note

1. Peter L. Benson, *All Kids Are Our Kids* (San Francisco, CA: Jossey-Bass), p. 40.

Greetings,

On Sunday, (date) we will be holding a Take It Home event at (time and location) for the first graders of our congregation and their parents entitled Family Service Projects. The purpose of this Take It Home Event is to inspire and engage the family to be the hands and feet of Christ through random acts of kindness, community service and missional living as a family.

As a part of the event, we would like to have you (wear your uniform) and share your testimony with the group. We only have 8 to 10 minutes for you to share your testimony so we would appreciate if you would succinctly focus on answering the following questions, remembering that your audience will be second graders and their parents.

- When and how did God call you into this position of servanthood?
- What has been one of your greatest experiences in serving others? Be specific.
- In what ways do you feel like you are doing God's work?
- How has serving others in this way brought you closer to God?

Following your testimony the group will have five minutes to ask you any questions they may have.

Thank you for considering this opportunity and if you have any questions feel free to contact me at (phone number and/or e-mail address). I look forward to hearing from you.

In Christ's Service,

Encouragement Cards

SIDE 1

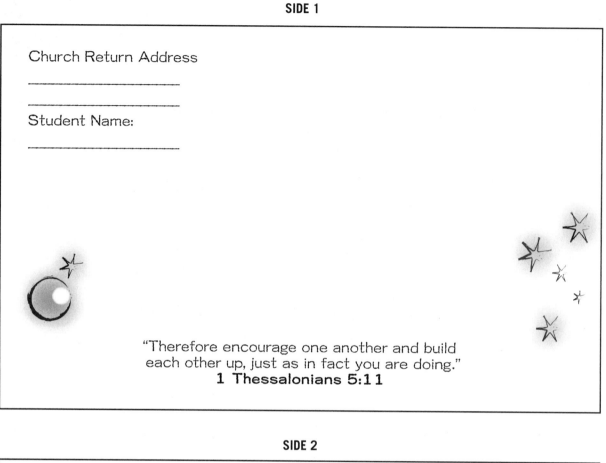

Church Return Address

_____

_____

Student Name:

_____

"Therefore encourage one another and build
each other up, just as in fact you are doing."
1 Thessalonians 5:11

SIDE 2

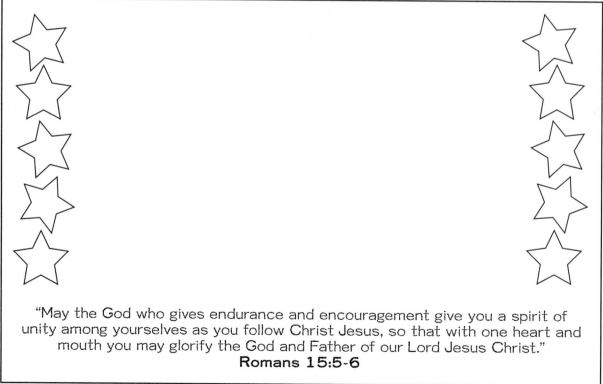

"May the God who gives endurance and encouragement give you a spirit of
unity among yourselves as you follow Christ Jesus, so that with one heart and
mouth you may glorify the God and Father of our Lord Jesus Christ."
Romans 15:5-6

Ways We Can Serve Our World

4

Family serve

A Little Book of Big Opportunities!

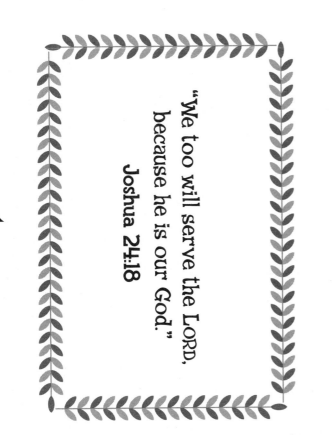

"We too will serve the LORD, because he is our God."

Joshua 24:18

1

Ways We Can Serve
Our Community

3

Ways We Can Serve
Our Church Family

2

Family Serve Calendar

MONTH

Our act of service this month will be:

"As for me and my household we will serve the LORD!" Joshua 24:15

Family Worship

Target Age of Children

Second Graders

Goal of Take It Home Event

To help families understand and appreciate the important role worship should play in their lives and to equip the family to worship at home.

Preparing for the Event

- Collect recordings of approximately 10 worship songs (see instructions in Name That Tune on p. 107).
- Arrange to interview your worship leader or a believer in your church who has had a long history of worshipping Jesus.
- Ask a family to lead a family worship time following the plan in Practice It on page 109. Let the family know how long you want the worship time to last.
- Make copies, at least five per family, of the Our Family Worship Worksheet (p. 112). Make a copy of the Preparation Guide (p. 113) for each family.
- Make copies, at least two per family, of the Car Time notes (p. 114).
- Have different instruments or pictures of the instruments in the room that the church has used to lead worship (e.g., organ, piano, guitar, bells, tambourines, drums, electric guitar, keyboard, bass guitar, harp).
- Collect a Bible, put paper and markers on tables and have a whiteboard and markers available. If your church uses bulletins for worship services, try to find some from previous years, dating as far back as you can. Place some on each table.

Event Outline

Explain It

Begin by reading this story as told by Mark Holmen.

"When I was a teenager, I dreaded the idea of having to get up and go to church on Sunday mornings. Sunday was my one day to sleep in and the idea of getting up early and having to dress up to attend a church service that was geared much more for the adults than for me was not something that excited me. Every Sunday morning the ritual would begin with my mom opening the door to the basement, which was where my bedroom was, and yelling in a very nice tone, 'Mark, time for you to get up and get ready for church.' Like clockwork my response was to respond, in a much grumpier way, 'Oh mom, do I have to go?' To which the response always was, 'Yes, Mark. Now let's get going.' This ritual went on for many months and even years until one Sunday something different happened which I will never forget.

"It began the same way, 'Mark, time for you to get up and get ready for church.' And I responded in kind, 'Oh mom, do I have to?' And this was when the change occurred. My mom responded with a different response, 'No Mark, you don't have to . . .' My ears could hardly believe what they had just heard! *Could this be? Is she serious?* There may actually be a God after all! And just

when my hopes were soaring at an all time high she completed the statement, 'No Mark, you don't have to go to church, you GET TO go to church.' My response? Stunned silence. I had no comeback and that was saying something for a teenage brat! And that statement has stuck with me for the rest of my life. 'Mark you don't have to go to church, you get to go to church.'"

Lead families in a time of discussion about their worship experiences. During the discussion, occasionally refer to the pictures displayed around the room and the bulletins set out on the tables. (If families are not already seated around tables, ask them to form family groups made up of several families.) Ask parents to share their experience with worship as they were growing up. "Did you and your family go to worship? If not, why not? If yes, what was it like? Did you ever have a 'have to' attitude regarding worship?" As a family, please share what you like most about coming to worship.

Then invite families to play a game of Name that Tune. Have a selection of 10 different worship songs ranging from traditional to contemporary ready to play. Have some easy ones like "Amazing Grace" and "Jesus Loves Me" so that everyone will hopefully get at least one right. Just for fun throw in a Christian rap or Christian rock song that not many will recognize. Play the first 10 to 15 seconds of each song and have each family try to come up with the title of each song and write it down.

Continue your explanation of worship, by asking a parent to read Psalm 150 aloud. Ask, "What is worship?" Write down the answers on the whiteboard. Ask, "How do we worship God? In what different ways have you worshipped God?" Let's look at how we worship God according to the Bible:

- Through reading God's Word (Colossians 4:16; 1 Thessalonians 5:27; 1 Timothy 4:13; Revelation 1:3);
- Through studying God's Word (Acts 6:2; 2 Timothy 2:15; 3:15);
- Through teaching God's Word (Acts 2:42; 6:7; 12:24; 18:28; 19:20; 1 Timothy 4:6; 2 Timothy 1:13; 2:2);
- Through preaching God's Word (2 Timothy 4:2);
- Through the singing of psalms, hymns and spiritual songs (Ephesians 5:19; Colossians 3:16; James 5:13);
- Through the lifting up of prayers and thanksgiving (Acts 2:42,46; 3:1; 4:31; Ephesians 6:18; Philippians 4:6; Colossians 4:2; 1 Thessalonians 5:17; 1 Timothy 2:1-2, 8);
- Through our praise (Hebrews 13:15);
- Through our good works (Hebrews 13:16).

Explain that worship is more than what we do on Sunday morning. Rick Warren in his book *Purpose-Driven Life* writes:

"Worship is not part of your life; it is your life. Worship is not just for church services. We are told to 'worship him continually' and to 'praise him from sunrise to sunset.' In the Bible people praised God at work, at home, in battle, in jail, and even in bed! Praise should be the first activity when you open your eyes in the morning and the last activity when you close them at night. This is the secret to a lifestyle of worship—doing everything as if you were doing it for Jesus."[1]

Inspire Them

Interview a worship leader of your church with questions such as:

- When did God call you to be a worship leader?
- For you, what is the purpose of worship?
- Why do we worship the way we do at our church?
- What are you hoping to accomplish through worship?
- What is the most exciting experience you have had leading worship?
- What parting words of wisdom or encouragement would you like to share with us regarding our worship life?

Or you may decide to interview a believer in your church with questions such as:

- How long have you been worshipping Jesus?
- What was worship like for you when you were a second grader?

- What is one of your favorite worship hymns or songs and why?
- What changes have you seen in worship over the years?
- What parting words of wisdom or encouragement would you like to share with us regarding our worship life?

Model It

Ask a family to model an abbreviated service based on the steps in Practice It.

Practice It

Let's put together a worship service that you can lead in your home. Explain the following steps to families:

Step 1—Establish a Theme

What is going to be the theme of your service? Is there something your family needs to focus on in worship? Theme examples are: God's love and forgiveness. Thankfulness. Treating others with mercy. Commitment to God. God's strength. Give each family the Our Family Worship Worksheet and Preparation Guide and allow them two to three minutes to determine the theme for their service. Ask families to write the theme on the worksheet.

Step 2—Select the Components of Your Service

Which components do you want in your service? Not all the components listed on your worksheet need to be included. As you explain each component listed on the worksheet, have families put a checkmark next to the components they want.

_____ Prayer

_____ Songs/Hymns (using worship CDs)

_____ Scripture Reading

_____ Sermon/Message (a Preparation Guide has been provided)

_____ Offering (give creative offering ideas such as each person completing the sentence "I'm thankful for . . .")

_____ Holy Communion

_____ Time of Silent Reflection and Confession

_____ Lord's Prayer

_____ Benediction/Blessing

_____ Announcements (It wouldn't be a worship service without announcements!)

Step 3—Put Together an Order of Service

Now that you have determined the components of your service, it's now time to put them together. How will your service start? What will follow that? How will the service end? Here is a sample order of service.

1. Opening Prayer

2. Two Worship Songs

3. Time of Offering

4. One Worship Song

5. Reading of Scripture

6. Message

7. Lord's Prayer

8. Closing Worship Song

As you can see, not all the components were used and some components were used multiple times like worship songs. It's your service, design it how you want! Give the families several minutes to plan and write the order for their service on their Our Family Worship Worksheet.

Step 4—Determine and Share the Leadership

Now it's time to determine who will be responsible for each part of the service. Who will select the songs? Who will select and read the scriptures? Who will give the message? Assign the different components of the service to different members of the family. (Note: A Preparation Guide [p. 113] has been provided to help you find Scripture and prepare a message.) For example:

1. Opening Prayer
   Kenny (third grader)

2. Two Worship Songs
   Lisa (teenager)

3. Time of Offering
   Kenny

4. One Worship Song
   Lisa

5. Reading of Scripture
   Laurie (mom)

6. Message
   Tedd and Laurie (parents)

7. Lord's Prayer
   Kenny

8. Closing Worship Song
   Lisa

Step 5—Set the Date, Time and Location for Your Service

When will you have your family worship service? What is the best location for the service?

Step 6—Invite Others to Attend

Is there anyone you want to invite to attend your service? The more the merrier!

Step 7—Worship as a Family!

You now have put together your first family worship service! Well done! Enjoy your service. When the service is complete, determine when your next family service will be and start the process over again.

Take It Home

To help you maintain an "I'm glad I get to go to worship" attitude in your family, we are providing you car time notes that you can use as a family as you go home from worship services at your church. God is continually speaking to us through worship, and the Car Time notes will help you discuss, as a family, how God spoke to you at worship. Hand out the Car Time notes.

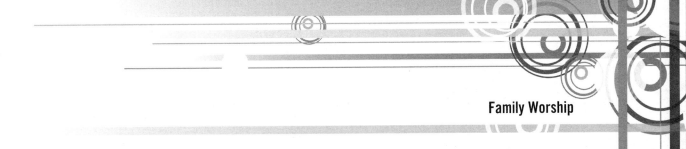

Suggested Resources

iExplore Music CD, Vols. 1 and 2. Ventura, CA: Gospel Light, 2007.

Find additional resources at www.faithbeginsathome.com.

Note

1. Rick Warren, *Purpose-Driven Life* (Grand Rapids, MI: Zondervan), pp. 63-67.

Step 1—Our family's worship theme will be _____.

Step 2—The components of our service will be:

_____ Prayer

_____ Songs/Hymns (using worship CDs)

_____ Scripture Reading (see Preparation Guide)

_____ Sermon/Message (see Preparation Guide)

_____ Offering

_____ Holy Communion

_____ Time of Silent Reflection and Confession

_____ Lord's Prayer

_____ Benediction/Blessing

_____ Announcements

Step 3—The order of our service will be:

_____

_____

_____

_____

_____

_____

_____

_____

Step 4—The person leading will be:

_____

_____

_____

_____

_____

_____

_____

_____

Step 5—The date, time and location of our service will be:

Step 6—Is there anyone you want to invite to attend your family's service?

Step 7—Worship as a family!

Most people don't have training in how to put together a sermon, but it's not as difficult as it may seem. Here are three simple rules to follow in putting together a sermon for your family worship service.

How Do I Find Scripture for Our Theme?

Once you have determined your theme, use a concordance to find Scripture that will shed light and truth on your theme. What's a concordance? A concordance is a ready reference found in most study Bibles that can be used in finding Scripture that relates to a specific name or topic. For example, if your family decides the theme of your worship should be sharing, you would look up the word sharing in your concordance, found usually at the back of your study Bible. Under the word "share," you would find the following Scripture passages:

1 Samuel 30:24 "All will share alike"

Luke 3:11 "The man with two tunics should share"

Hebrews 13:16 "To do good and to share with others"

As you look up the Scripture passages, let the Word of God speak truth to you and simply share that truth with your family.

Start with the Biblical Foundation (God's Story): Begin your message by examining what the Bible says about the topic or theme of your service. Complete this sentence: "What I understand the Bible to be saying about this topic or theme is . . ."

Add Personal Inspiration (My Story): What does this mean to me personally? How does or has this Biblical truth impacted me or someone else I know personally? Use personal stories, examples or illustrations to make your point.

Close with Practical Application (Our Story): What does this truth mean for us as a family? How do we apply this truth/teaching to our lives?

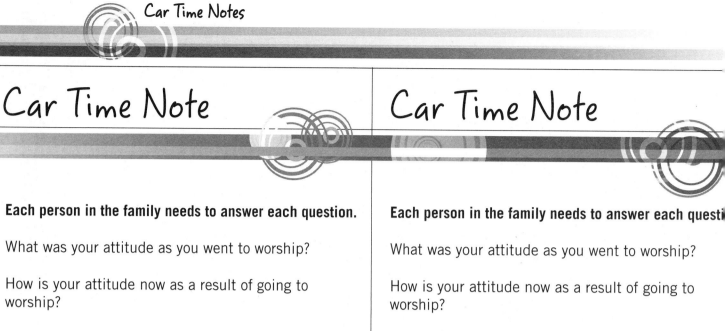

Car Time Note

Each person in the family needs to answer each question.

What was your attitude as you went to worship?

How is your attitude now as a result of going to worship?

What was your favorite part of the worship service?

What was the message God spoke to you through your worship?

How can you apply that message to your everyday life?

Car Time Note

Each person in the family needs to answer each question.

What was your attitude as you went to worship?

How is your attitude now as a result of going to worship?

What was your favorite part of the worship service?

What was the message God spoke to you through your worship?

How can you apply that message to your everyday life?

Car Time Note

Each person in the family needs to answer each question.

What was your attitude as you went to worship?

How is your attitude now as a result of going to worship?

What was your favorite part of the worship service?

What was the message God spoke to you through your worship?

How can you apply that message to your everyday life?

Car Time Note

Each person in the family needs to answer each question.

What was your attitude as you went to worship?

How is your attitude now as a result of going to worship?

What was your favorite part of the worship service?

What was the message God spoke to you through your worship?

How can you apply that message to your everyday life?

My Bible

Target Age of Children

Third Graders

Goal of Take It Home Event

To empower families to spend time together reading the Bible and memorizing Scripture, truly putting God's Word at the center of their lives.

Preparing for the Event

- Set up and collect supplies for the Bible Trivia game. Make a copy of Bible Trivia Questions (pp. 121-122).
- Order a Bible for each child.
- Make a copy of the Bible Presentation Sample Letter (p. 123) for each family.
- Have materials on hand for making Bible covers (see Model It). Provide several copies of the Bible Cover Instructions page (p. 124).
- Make a copy of Key Scripture Verses for Our Family (pp. 125-126) for each family.
- Collect Bibles and have available a whiteboard and markers.

Event Outline

Explain It

Let parents compete against kids in some good old Bible trivia! Place a whiteboard up front and on one side write "Parents" and on the other "Kids." This event will not only be fun, but also an opportunity to teach some basic things about the Bible while having a blast doing it! Collect these items and then get ready to play: game show host costume (wig, glasses and sport coat), two Bibles that match the ones you will give out later), a small table, a tennis ball, Bible Trivia Questions page.

Bible Quiz Show Script

Enthusiastically introduce the host of the show, "Mr. Billy-Bob Bible Boy!" but he doesn't enter.

Repeat the introduction "Mr. Billy-Bob Bible Boy!" but again, he doesn't come out.

Excuse yourself from the room as if there is a problem and you need to go and look for the host. Then, quickly change into your costume and yell from the hall (or changing room), "Mr. Billy-Bob Bible Boy!" Come running in with the costume on. And now, using a new voice, host the Bible Quiz Show (referring to it as BQS).

Bible Quiz Show Instructions

Stand with the small table in front of you (see sketch).

Ask for one child and one adult volunteer to come forward.

Place the tennis ball and the two Bibles on the table.

Have the two contestants stand on either side of the table.

After you read a question from Bible Trivia Questions page, the first contestant to grab the tennis ball off the table will have an opportunity to answer the question.

If contestant gets the answer wrong, the other contestant will have an opportunity to answer

If you ask contestants to find a specific verse in the Bible instead of answering a question, the contestants will grab the Bibles and look up the verse. The first contestant to successfully find the verse and then grab the tennis ball wins that round.

After a set time or number of questions, conclude the trivia game. Move into the Scripture teaching about what the Bible is and how we are to use it.

Scripture Teaching

Second Timothy 3:16 says, "All Scripture is God-breathed and is useful for teaching, rebuking, correcting and training in righteousness, so that the man of God may be thoroughly equipped for every good work." Discuss this Scripture as follows:

"God-breathed." Have a family look up Genesis 2:7. The Bible is alive in the same way that we are alive, because we have the breath of God breathed into us. Have a family look up John 1:1. Jesus is the Word incarnate, God's Word in human form. Have a family look up Hebrews 4:12. The Bible is living, on the move, doing things in the lives of people.

"Useful for teaching." What are some of the things the Bible teaches us? (Who God is; how Jesus lived and what He taught; what it means to be a part of God's family, the Church; how we can gain salvation, how we should act, how God has worked in the lives of people throughout history.) Can anyone think of a story Jesus tells and what it teaches us?

"Rebuking, correcting." What does it mean that the Bible rebukes or corrects us? When do we need to be rebuked or corrected?

"Training, equipping." Who are people that typically need to go into train-

ing? (Athletes—1 Corinthians 9:24-27; Soldiers—Ephesians 6:13-17.)

"Therefore put on the full armor of God, so that when the day of evil comes, you may be able to stand your ground, and after you have done everything, to stand. Stand firm then, with the belt of truth buckled around your waist, with the breastplate of righteousness in place, and with your feet fitted with the readiness that comes from the gospel of peace. In addition to all this, take up the shield of faith, with which you can extinguish all the flaming arrows of the evil one. Take the helmet of salvation and the sword of the Spirit, which is the word of God" (Ephesians 6:13-17).

Have a child come forward. Ask, "What are some things from this passage that the Bible trains us in?" As people give answers, pantomime strapping on the appropriate gear to your volunteer soldier.

- Belt = Truth. The Bible trains us in becoming people of truth;
- Breastplate = Righteousness. The Bible trains us to be people right before God;
- Boots = Peace. The Bible trains us to be people who have God's peace;
- Shield = Faith. The Bible trains us to be people who live by faith;
- Helmet = Salvation. The Bible trains us to walk in the light of our salvation;
- Sword = Bible. The Bible trains

117

us to use God's Word effectively to advance the Kingdom of God.

Inspire Them

Begin by telling this story from Dave Teixeira.

"A professor of a photography class I took in college gave us the task of taking some pictures of what was most important to us in life, photos that would describe who we were and who we wanted to become. As I sat and thought about what I would shoot all I could think of was taking pictures of my Bible. And that's what I did. I had that Bible in flowerbeds, on tables, lying on a bed of rocks and even propped up against the cross. You see, when I began to read it consistently the Bible went from being 'that book' to 'my book.' It became a part of me, who I was and who I was becoming."

This is what this Take It Home Event is all about. It is about empowering you as families to transform who you and your children are by making "the Bible" into "your Bible." Ask everyone to relax, to sit back and close their eyes. Read for them a passage from Jesus' Sermon on the Mount found in Matthew 5:1-12:

"Now when he saw the crowds, he went up on a mountainside and sat down. His disciples came to him, and he began to teach them saying: 'Blessed are the poor in spirit, for theirs is the kingdom of heaven. Blessed are those who mourn, for they will be comforted. Blessed are the meek, for they will inherit the earth. Blessed are those who hunger and thirst for righteousness, for they will be filled. Blessed are the merciful, for they will be shown mercy. Blessed are the pure in heart, for they will see God. Blessed are the peacemakers, for they will be called sons of God. Blessed are those who are persecuted because of righteousness, for theirs is the kingdom of heaven. Blessed are you when people insult you, persecute you and falsely say all kinds of evil against you because of me. Rejoice and be glad, because great is your reward in heaven, for in the same way they persecuted the prophets who were before you.'"

When you have finished the reading, ask the group how their attitude, perspective and interactions with others would change if they read that passage each morning before they started their day.

The Bible changes us. It has a way of transforming us into people who don't just act more like Christ, but who are more like Christ.

Model It

Separate parents from the kids. Give parents the Bibles you have picked out to give to the children of your church. Ask parents to open to the presentation page in the front of the Bible. On this page there should be space to write who the Bible is from, who it is for and the date it was given. Have the parents write their child's name in the "Presented To" slot, the appropriate date and their name(s) in the "Presented By" space. Explain that the role of the church is to empower parents, helping them fulfill the spiritual responsibilities they have with their children. (Note: Many churches have parents promise to put the Scriptures in the hands of their children when the child is baptized or dedicated, and this is a very practical chance for the church to help parents keep their promise to personally place the Bible in the hands of their child.)

Give each parent a copy of the Bible Presentation Sample Letter. Have the parent(s) write a letter to their children in the front cover of the Bible.

While the parents write in the Bibles, have the children decorate a cover for the Bible they are soon to receive. Depending on your church's budget you can use paper from your church's supply room or special Bible covers with pockets and zippers. Provide Bible Cover Instructions page, markers, paper, scissors, glue, crayons, paint, stickers, etc. whatever kids will enjoy decorating their Bible covers with. Later, as the kids put their new Bibles into the covers they have made, you can talk to them about the significance this represents in not just having *a* Bible, but *my* Bible.

Children may also make and decorate bookmarks for their Bibles if they have additional time. Parents may write their favorite Bible verse on a bookmark to present to their kids along with the Bible.

Practice It

Lead families in a Bible Presentation Ceremony. Have parents place hands on their children and repeat, phrase by phrase:

> _____ you are my child and I am very proud of you.

> You are a wonderful creation of God who is fearfully and wonderfully made (Psalm 139:14).

> God has a special plan for your life, a plan for hope and a future (Jeremiah 29:11).

> May this book be a lamp unto your feet (Psalm 119:105).

> May it penetrate your soul (Hebrews 4:12).

> May it teach you, correct you and train you (2 Timothy 3:16) to be the very person God longs for you to be.

> We love you and present to you your very own Bible.

Allow time for kids to read the letters their parents wrote in the front of the Bible or have parents read the letters aloud to their child.

Then have the kids remain standing with their Bibles and their Bible covers and repeat after you phrase by phrase:

> I receive this Bible

> as God's Word for me.

> I will strive to know and
>   understand it

and through it know God.

May it shape my character,

penetrate my soul,

direct my decisions,

shepherd my heart,

be a beacon of truth,

and lead my life.

This is MY BIBLE!

Instruct the students to place their personal covers on the Bible as a symbol of it truly being God's Word for them.

Close this time by asking parents to place hands on their children and pray for them.

Take It Home

Give each family the Key Scripture Verses for our Family that provides a list of Scriptures that their family can look up, underline or highlight in their Bibles, and memorize together, and includes Bible activities they can do at home.

Suggested Resources

Blankenbaker, Frances. *What the Bible Is All About for Young Explorers*. Ventura, CA: Gospel Light, 1986.

The Adventure Bible. Grand Rapids, MI: Zonderkidz, 2000.

The Big Book of Bible Facts and Fun. Ventura, CA: Gospel Light, 2005.

Find additional resources at www.faithbeginsathome.com.

1. The Bible is broken into two main sections. What are they called? **(Old Testament and New Testament.)**

2. Name the first five books of the Bible. **(Genesis, Exodus, Leviticus, Numbers, Deuteronomy.)**

Bonus: What are these first five books of the Old Testament called? **(Pentateuch—*penta* means "five" and *teuchos* means "scroll." These books are also called the Torah which means the Book of the Law.)**

3. How many official disciples did Jesus have? **(Twelve.)**

Bonus: Name two of Jesus' disciples. **(See Matthew 10:2-4: Simon, Andrew, James, John, Philip, Bartholomew, Thomas, Matthew, James, Thaddaeus, Simon the Zealot, Judas.)**

4. Name four fruits of the Holy Spirit given in Galatians 5:22-23. **(See Galatians 5:22-23: love, joy, peace, patience, kindness, goodness, faithfulness, gentleness, self-control.)**

5. What are the two things Jesus claims as one in His answer to the question, "Which is the greatest commandment in the law?" **(See Matthew 22:36-40:**

"Love the Lord your God with all your heart and with all your soul and with all your mind" and "Love your neighbor as yourself.")

6. How many books in the Bible are considered "Gospels" and what are their names? **(Matthew, Mark, Luke and John.)**

7. What were the names of Jesus' mother and father on earth? **(Mary and Joseph.)**

Bonus: What was the name of the town Jesus was born in? **(Bethlehem.)**

8. Who was Isaac's father? **(Abraham.)**

Bonus: Which of Isaac's son's wrestled with God? **(Jacob.)**

9. Why did Joseph end up in Egypt? **(His brothers sold him into slavery.)**

10. Moses heard the voice of God come out of what? **(A burning bush.)**

Bonus: When Moses asked God His name, what was his reply? **(*Yahweh*.)**

11. What was the name of the first king of Israel? **(Saul.)**

12. What was the name of the giant that the second king of

Israel killed when he was a boy? **(Goliath.)**

Bonus: What did he use to kill him? **(Sling and stone.)**

13. Who in the Bible was swallowed by a whale? **(Jonah.)**

Bonus: What was the country Jonah desperately did not want to go and share the message of God's love with? **(Nineveh.)**

14. The night before His arrest, Jesus celebrated the Passover meal with His disciples. What act of service did He perform before the meal began? **(Washed the disciples' feet.)**

15. Although Jesus was born in Bethlehem, He was raised in a different town. What town was it? Hint: He was often referred to as Jesus of ____. **(Nazareth.)**

16. One of the miracles we read about Jesus performing is Him walking on the water out to His disciple in a boat on the Sea of Galilee. Which disciple also walked on water that day? **(Peter.)**

17. In Matthew 7 Jesus tells a parable of two house builders. What are the two surfaces or foundations on which they build their houses? **(Sand and rock.)**

18. In the Book of Acts, a Pharisee who strongly opposed the newly forming Christian Church encountered Christ and was converted. What was his name before and after his conversion? **(Saul, Paul.)**

Bonus: Where was Paul when he encountered Christ? **(Road to Damascus.)**

19. After becoming a Christ-follower, Paul began to share the good news of salvation in Christ with what group of people? **(Gentiles.)**

20. In which of Paul's letters does he instruct the believers to imitate Christ's humility using these words: "Each of you should look not only to your own interests, but also to the interests of others. Your attitude should be the same as that of Christ Jesus." **(Philippians. See Philippians 2:4-5.)**

Dear (name),

You are such a blessing to our family and this world. God has given you so many special gifts and we see those in you already. Our prayer is that by drawing close to God, through the Scriptures, you will become the young (man or woman) God longs for you to be. We know that if you invest time with God through His Word, that you will be changed. We have confidence in this because the Bible has a way of transforming us, accomplishing in us what God desires (see Isaiah 55:11).

Our prayer is that you would become a person in whom the Word of God dwells richly. God promises that He has a plan for you and that if you follow Him you will have a hope and a future (see Jeremiah 29:11). We love you and know that through God you can and will become all He intends for you to be.

Love,

Mom & Dad

crease

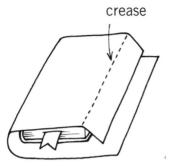

1. Set your closed Bible between a paper you have folded in half. Make sharp folds around the edges of the Bible.

3"

2. Take out the Bible and open the paper. Draw a line about 3 inches (7.5 cm) all the way around the fold lines. Cut on the line.

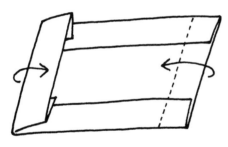

3. Fold the paper along the top and bottom. Then fold the sides of the paper.

4. Insert the front cover of your Bible into the opening on the left of the cover. Do the same thing with the right side.

slide
the back
cover

5. Decorate your cover!

124

Scriptures to Read

Hebrews 4:12

"For the word of God is living and active. Sharper than any double-edged sword, it penetrates even to dividing soul and spirit, joints and marrow; it judges the thoughts and attitudes of the heart."

Psalm 119:105

"Your word is a lamp to my feet and a light for my path."

Isaiah 55:11

"So is my word that goes out from my mouth: It will not return to me empty, but will accomplish what I desire and achieve the purpose for which I sent it."

Psalm 119:11

"I have hidden your word in my heart that I might not sin against you."

2 Timothy 3:15-17 (NLT)

"You have been taught the holy Scriptures from childhood, and they have given you the wisdom to receive the salvation that comes by trusting in Christ Jesus. All Scripture is inspired by God and is useful to teach us what is true and to make us realize what is wrong in our lives. It corrects us when we are wrong and teaches us to do what is right. God uses it to prepare and equip his people to do every good work."

Family Bible Activities

1. Read the story of the wise and foolish builders in Matthew 7:24-29 and discuss it together.

What is Jesus teaching us in this story?

What do the rain, streams and winds represent?

How can you build your house on the rock?

2. Look up and highlight these verses in your Bibles:

Genesis 28:15

1 Kings 2:3

Isaiah 40:31

Jeremiah 29:11

Proverbs 3:5-6

Psalm 119:11

Matthew 10:2-4

Matthew 22:36-40

John 3:16

John 20:31

Romans 8:38-39

Galatians 2:20

Galatians 5:22

3. Get to know your Bible.

Get familiar with the Table of Contents. Take turns selecting a verse in the Bible and having the others find it in their Bibles.

Read "About the Bible" (one of the beginning pages)

Read "About the Old Testament Books" (one of the beginning pages)

Read "About the New Testament Books" (located between the Old and New Testaments)

Choose one of the listed "Illustrations," find its page and read it as a family.

Choose a map and talk about it

Money and Me

Target Age of Children

Fourth and Fifth Graders

Goal of Take It Home Event

To learn what Jesus has to say about money, be challenged to consider how God might shape their finances and be empowered to develop some God-honoring and freedom-building money management skills at home.

Preparing for the Event

- Set up the activity stations as described in Explain It and make a copy of the Station Ballot (pp. 135-136) on card stock for each family.
- Purchase several small prizes (gift certificate for ice cream, a board game, etc.) to be given to the families who receive the most points.
- Make a copy of the Bible Discovery page (pp. 137-138) for each family.
- Make several copies of The Allowance Challenge (p. 139) for each family.
- Collect a Bible for each family, pens or pencils and have a whiteboard and markers available.

Event Outline

Explain It

As families arrive, give them a Station Ballot and pen or pencil. Instruct families to rotate from station to station, starting at any station they wish. (Optional: Depending on the number of families attending this Take It Home Event, you may want to group several families together. Assign each group a station at which to start. Each family group rotates together.) At each station families will use their ballot to record their answers, guesses, times, etc. and the number of points they earn. Some stations require a leader to be present. At other stations you may simply provide the instructions for families to follow.

Give families the time by which all 10 stations need to be completed. Tell them that the family who receives the most points will receive a prize!

Station 1—The Jar

Fill a jar with a variety of pennies, nickels, dimes, quarters and a few dollar bills. Have each family group guess: (1) How many nickels and pennies are in the jar? (2) What is the total value of just the dimes in the jar? (3) How much money is in this jar? Announce answers and award points before the family groups move on to the next center.

SCORING FOR STATION 1

Closest guess for each question receives 10 points.

Station 2—People We See

Pin $1, $5, $10, $20 and $100 dollar bills on a display board. Provide a list of these presidents: George Washington (1st U.S. President), Thomas Jefferson (3rd U.S. President), Abraham Lincoln (16th U.S. President), Alexander Hamilton (1st Secretary of the Treasury), Andrew Jackson (7th U.S. President), Ulysses Grant (18th U.S. President), Ben Franklin (Statesman). Have families match the bill with the name of the person pictured on that bill.

ANSWERS AND SCORING FOR STATION 2

$1—George Washington

$5—Abraham Lincoln

$10—Alexander Hamilton

$20—Andrew Jackson

$100—Ben Franklin

Each correct answer receives 10 points. Award a bonus 10 points if all answers are correct.

Stations 3 to 5—Money Math

Each of these stations will require a stopwatch and both play money and real money. Collect the following amount of money in separate resealable baggies: a $10 bill (play money), a $5 bill (play money), three $1 bills (play or real money), four quarters, five dimes, four nickels, five pennies. Make a bag for each child. Have a leader at each station.

When the money has been distributed, tell children that they will be

asked to answer a question at each station. If kids get stuck, their parents can help them. At each station, leader asks questions and times the responses.

Question for Station 3: An item costs $13.22 and is paid for with a $20 bill. What is the amount of change that should be given?

Question for Station 4: A parent buys two candy bars for their child at 75 cents each and pays with a $10 bill. What is the amount of change that should be given?

Question for Station 5: What is 10 percent of the total amount of money you have, excluding pennies?

ANSWERS AND SCORING FOR STATIONS 3 TO 5.

Station 3: $6.78 ($5, $1, two quarters, two dimes, one nickel, three pennies).

The correct answer receives 10 points

Station 4: $8.50 ($5, three $1, two quarters or five dimes).

The correct answer receives 10 points.

Station 5: $19.70 x .10 = $1.97

The correct answer receives 10 points.

Optional: If several families are at these stations at the same time, award a bonus 10 points to the family who is able to answer the fastest.

Station 6—Can't Break a Dollar
Ask families to answer this question, "Using only coins, what is the largest possible amount of money you can have without being able to make change for a dollar?"

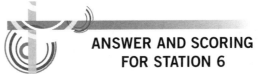

ANSWER AND SCORING FOR STATION 6

$1.19 (three quarters, four dimes, four pennies).

Correct answer receives 10 points.

Station 7—What You're Made Of
Have a dollar bill at this station for the kids to feel. Explain that paper money is made primarily of two fabrics. Ask families to decide the answer to the question, "Which of the following three answers correctly describes its make-up?" (a) 25% Cotton, 75% Linen; (b) 25% Linen, 75% Cotton; (c) mostly made of silk.

ANSWER AND SCORING FOR STATION 7

B is the correct answer.

Correct answer receives 10 points.

Station 8—Go the Extra Mile
At the same time, have two or more families estimate the answer to this question, "If pennies were laid side by side for a mile, how many would there be?"

ANSWER AND SCORING FOR STATION 8

84,480 pennies

Closest guess receives 10 points.

Station 9—Flip It

Have a table set up with several coins. Flip a coin four times, letting it come to rest on the table surface (coins that land in your hand or on the ground don't count and should be reflipped). Record the number of "heads" and "tails" you end up with.

SCORING FOR STATION 9

All four flips were "tails" receives 30 points.

All four flips were "heads" receives 30 points.

Two flips were "heads" and two flips were "tails" receives 10 points.

Station 10—Groovy

Place several quarters and dimes on a table in this center. Have a leader ready to give instructions and call time after three minutes. At the same time, have two or more families guess the number of grooves on the edge of a quarter and on the edge of a dime. Tell families they can work on coming up with their correct answer until you call time. You should give a 10-second warning before their answer to the question must be written down. They will have until then

to do some groove counting if they choose.

ANSWER AND SCORING FOR STATION 10

A quarter has 119 grooves.

A dime has 118 grooves.

Closest guesses receive 10 points.

After completing this opening activity, gather families together and comment on how money is a topic that everyone seems to want to talk about. Money experts are common. Explain that the Bible also talks about money. Ask, "Why does the Bible talk about money so much?" After several volunteers respond, comment that money is powerful. The more powerful something is the more care and instruction we need as we prepare to use it.

Read this story from Dave Teixeira.

"When I was a kid, I remember doing yard work with my Dad. From my perspective it seemed like I always got the really boring jobs while he had all the fun. I had to rake leaves while he got to use the cool blower machine. I had to sweep grass while he used the electric weed-whacker. I had to pick up pinecones while he got to use the lawnmower. One day I asked my dad why he got to use all the fun power tools and I had to do all the manual labor. He explained to me that all the machines he was using were very powerful and could be very dangerous if handled incorrectly. Using this equipment required maturity, training and extreme care."

Although it might not seem like it, money is a lot like lawn tools. It is powerful and when handled incorrectly it can be very dangerous. Money is a key battle you will fight. In some ways, your life is like a war that is being fought. The goal of this war is to win your heart, your soul. And just like in other wars, in this war there are also key battles. And, believe it or not, Jesus talked about one of these key battles in the war for your soul. It's called the "Treasure Battle!"

A war is made up of a bunch of smaller conflicts called battles. When you add up the results of all the battles that have been fought, you will get a pretty good idea of who wins the war. But some battles are bigger than others. Some battles are more significant, more influential in determining the outcome of the war. These key battles have the power to shift and change the momentum of the entire war.

For example, think about the Civil War. What is generally considered the key battle of the Civil War? (The Battle of Gettysburg.) The Battle of Gettysburg was fought from July 1-3, 1863 in what was then a small crossroads town in south-central Pennsylvania. This battle was a major turning point in the Civil War. For three days 165,000 men fought there and 51,000 of them became casualties in defense of their beliefs.

Matthew 6:19-24 describes a key battle in our lives. Read the passage aloud:

"Do not store up for yourselves treasures on earth, where moth and rust destroy, and where thieves break in and steal. But store up for yourselves treasures in heaven, where moth and rust do not destroy, and where thieves do not break in and steal. For where your treasure is, there your heart will be also. The eye is the lamp of the body. If your eyes are good, your whole body will be full of light. But if your eyes are bad, your whole body will be full of darkness. If then the light within you is darkness, how great is that darkness! No one can serve two masters. Either he will hate the one and love the other, or he will be devoted to the one and despise the other. You cannot serve both God and Money."

So, why is this Treasure Battle so key? Why does it really matter where your treasure is? (See vs. 21.) It is really a battle for your heart. What does it mean to have your heart somewhere? You will find your heart in what you love and what you really care about.

When Jesus is asked what the greatest commandment is, what does He say? In Matthew 22:37 Jesus replied, "Love the Lord your God with all your heart, and with all your soul and with all your mind. This is the first and greatest commandment."

So God wants to be the love of our hearts! We know that where our treasure is, there our hearts will be also.

Does this mean we are not allowed to like money at all? God has given us money for use and enjoyment. All that we have is a gift from Him, including money, and God says you are allowed to enjoy it. Ask, "How many of you sometimes get money in your birthday cards? Are you ever so eager to open the card to see if there's money that you forget to look at the card?"

Read verse 24 again: "You cannot serve both God and Money." What God is saying is that we must never love and serve money. Money should never be more important than God.

Use a whiteboard to illustrate and explain the proper place God wants to occupy in our lives. Draw a large circle and explain that this circle represents our lives. Explain that there are many things that are a part of each of our lives.

Ask the families to share some things that are a part of their lives and write the words inside the circle. Examples might include: family, friends, school, work, sports, church, God, money, video games, dance, vacation, chores, kids, television, computer, food.

When the crowd has caught on and the circle is starting to fill up, draw a chair or throne in the center of the circle. Explain that there is always something that is the focus of your life, something that's in charge, something that everything else in your life submits to. Whatever that thing is, it's on the throne.

According to Jesus and the first and greatest commandment, who should be on the throne of your life? God! Do you sometimes feel like friends are becoming more important than God? Sports? Schoolwork? For parents it might be work, bills, schedule, yard work, cleaning, or your kids.

Jesus is warning us not that money is evil, but that we can allow it to become king and push God off the throne.

So how can we keep a right perspective? Remember this: It's all God's. Who made the world? Who made you? Who made the trees we use to make money? Who gave you the ability to do things to earn that money? Everything is God's!

Give it away. If you had $100 of your own that you earned and I told you that today you had to give half of it away to needy people it might be hard. You might be saying, "but I earned this money to buy a new computer." But if I gave you $100 of my money and told you to give away half to needy people, you would be pumped up and enthusiastic for two reasons. First of all, you would have a blast giving money to needy people and watching their faces light up as they received your gift. But second, you would do some quick math and you would realize that you were going to be able to keep $50 for yourself. And that is how we need to see our money. It's money God has given us and we should enjoy passing His money along to others and also be excited that He is letting us keep some of it for ourselves!

Remember, it's only stuff. There is a story about a wealthy guy, a guy who had tons of money. When he died, the angels came down to escort him up to heaven. But when they told him that he could NOT bring anything with him he insisted that he bring a suitcase he had packed full of gold bars. "No way!" the angels said, "absolutely nothing can come with." But the man insisted. Arriving at the pearly gates of heaven, Saint Peter greeted the gentleman but told him that he would have to inspect the contents of his suitcase. Opening the bag, Peter became very perplexed and asked the gentleman, "Why in the world are you lugging around street pavement?" Here is the point. While money may seem very important when we consider it from a worldly perspective, when it is seen from a heavenly or eternal perspective, it is really nothing at all. The most valuable things on earth are literally street pavement for all eternity in heaven.

Inspire Them

Read this story from Dave Teixeira.

"The truths in Matthew 6:19-20 became so real to me recently when I was down in southern Mississippi following the devastation of hurricane Katrina. Here were miles and miles of houses that had literally been destroyed along with everything in them. People had lost all they had. And all I could think was, 'Man, earthly treasure is so easily destroyed.' The thief had broken into the lives of these people in the form of a hurricane and stolen all their earthly treasure."

This loss of earthly treasure will happen to all of us. At some point, in some way, we will all be robbed of our earthly treasures and we better have some treasure stored up someplace more secure. We better have some treasure stored up in eternal things. We better have some treasure stored up with God because that is treasure that can never be stolen. That is treasure that is protected and secure!

Model It

Give families a copy of the Bible Discovery page. Assign families a few of the verses to read and talk about what they mean. Then ask them to share some of the things they discovered about God's perspective on money.

Practice It

Give families a copy of the book *The Secret of Handling Money God's Way* (see Suggested Resources on p. 134). Have families work together to complete Chapter 1 and challenge them over the next few months to complete the remaining 11 chapters. You may want to provide some incentive for families who complete the workbook (half off summer camp fee to the first student who turns in a completed workbook, quarter off summer camp fee to the second student who turns in a completed workbook and $25 gift card to a local electronics store for the third student).

Take It Home

Give your parents several copies of The Allowance Challenge. Encourage them to provide ways their children can earn some consistent income. Now, as soon as your kids hear you tell their parents to give them money, they are going to love you. Remind them of the key word in that sentence, "Earn." Tell parents to talk to their kids about what they are doing with the money they receive and why.

Suggested Resources

Dayton, Howard and Bev Dayton. *The Secret of Handling Money God's Way*. Chicago, IL: Moody Publishers, 2003.

Find additional resources at www.faithbeginsathome.com.

STATION BALLOT

○ STATION 1: THE JAR

- How many nickels and pennies are in the jar?
- What is the total value of just the dimes in the jar?
- How much money is in this jar?

_____

_____

_____

○ STATION 2: PEOPLE WE SEE

Match the bill with the name of the person pictured on the bill.

$1	Ben Franklin
$5	Alexander Hamilton
$10	Andrew Jackson
$20	George Washington
$100	Abraham Lincoln

○ STATION 3: MONEY MATH

An item costs $13.22 and is paid for with a $20 bill. What is the amount of change that should be given?

_____

_____

_____

○ STATION 4: MONEY MATH

A parent buys two candy bars for their child at 75 cents each and pays with a $10 bill. What is the amount of change that should be given?

_____

_____

_____

○ STATION 5: MONEY MATH

What is 10 percent of the total amount of money you have, excluding pennies?

_____

_____

STATION BALLOT

○ STATION 6: CAN'T BREAK A DOLLAR

Using only coins, what is the largest possible amount of money you can have without being able to make change for a dollar?

_____

_____

_____

○ STATION 7: WHAT YOU'RE MADE OF

Which of the follow three answers correctly describe the makeup of a dollar bill?

(a) 25% Cotton, 75% Linen
(b) 25% Linen, 75% Cotton
(c) mostly made of silk

○ STATION 8: GO THE EXTRA MILE

If pennies were laid side by side for a mile, how many would there be?

_____

_____

_____

○ STATION 9: FLIP IT

Flip a coin four times, letting it come to rest on the table surface. Record the number of "heads" and "tails" you end up with.

Heads: _____
Tails: _____

○ STATION 10: GROOVY

Guess the number of grooves on the edge of a quarter and on the edge of a dime.

Quarter: _____
Dime: _____

Deuteronomy 8:18

"But remember the LORD your God, for it is he who gives you the ability to produce wealth, and so confirms his covenant, which he swore to your forefathers, as it is today."

Ecclesiastes 5:10

"Whoever loves money never has money enough; whoever loves wealth is never satisfied with his income."

Matthew 19:24

"Again I tell you, it is easier for a camel to go through the eye of a needle than for a rich man to enter the kingdom of God."

1 Timothy 6:17-19

"Command those who are rich in this present world not to be arrogant nor to put their hope in wealth, which is so uncertain, but to put their hope in God, who richly provides us with everything for our enjoyment. Command them to do good, to be rich in good deeds, and to be generous and willing to share. In this way they will lay up treasure for themselves as a firm foundation for the coming age, so that they may take hold of the life that is truly life."

Proverbs 11:4

"Wealth is worthless in the day of wrath, but righteousness delivers from death."

Proverbs 11:28

"Whoever trusts in his riches will fall, but the righteous will thrive like a green leaf."

Proverbs 15:16

"Better a little with the fear of the LORD than great wealth with turmoil."

Proverbs 22:2

"Rich and poor have this in common: The LORD is the Maker of them all."

Proverbs 23:4-5

"Do not wear yourself out to get rich; have the wisdom to show restraint. Cast but a glance at riches, and they are gone, for they will surely sprout wings and fly off to the sky like an eagle."

Proverbs 28:20

"A faithful man will be richly blessed, but one eager to get rich will not go unpunished."

Proverbs 28:22

"A stingy man is eager to get rich and is unaware that poverty awaits him."

The Allowance Challenge

Name: _____ Age: _____ Month: _____

My Income	
Income from Allowance	
Income from Gifts	
Income from Extra Chores	

My Plan	
What I Will Spend	
What I Will Save	
What I Will Give (Tithe) to Help Others	

My Records Write down the ways you followed your plan.	
Week 1	
Week 2	
Week 3	
Week 4	

Computer Boundaries

Target Age of Children

Teenagers

Goal of Take It Home Event

To empower parents and give them the information and tools that will help them effectively support and guide their children into good, safe, Christ-honoring decisions on the computer as they spend time online.

Preparing for the Event

- Determine how you will schedule this event. If you have a large group, divide parents and teens into two groups and present the material twice on separate nights. You may also be tempted to ask the question, "Should we have parents and teens or just parents?" There are several practical reasons for having parents with teens. First, it is simply good for parents and kids to have shared experiences. In a world that keeps us so busy and often separates families, the church should take every opportunity to bring families together. Second, meeting together will help with communication. It gets parents and kids on the same page, speaking the same language. It also saves Mom from having to say, "Pastor Dave said. . . ." When parents and kids hear the same information, it provides a common ground—a jumping off place from which to begin discussion. Finally, and most importantly, the kids will really add to this event. Who knows better what is happening in the teen cyber world than teens? You will be surprised at how helpful your kids will be in guiding parents, giving tips and offering suggestions on how to regulate and interact with them about computer use. A classic line you are likely to hear at this event will go something like this, "You can try that but a lot of kids at my school. . . ." Get your families together and let them talk, learn and have fun.

- Determine how you will lead this event. A big part of this event is the hands-on experience of getting families online and exploring some things together. This can happen in one of three ways. Choose which one of the following options will work best in your situation for the Virtual Tour (see pp. 144-145). **Option 1:** The best option, but probably the most difficult to accomplish, is to have an Internet-accessed computer in front of each family. One way of making this happen is to use a computer lab room at a nearby school or library. One leader can guide families through an online tour and they will actually be able to have a hands-on experience. **Option 2:** Set up stations, each manned with a computer and a guide. At each station families will gather around, explore, learn and ask about one aspect of computer life. After an allotted time at each station, families rotate until everyone has experienced each station. This approach works well because each station will be dealing with smaller groups and people will be able to ask more personalized questions. **Option 3:** Guide your entire group through the tour together by hooking up one computer to a projection screen and having everyone watch as you drive through the virtual world.

- Invite a computer expert—someone who is knowledgeable in getting around on the computer—to attend this event. You may want to consider contacting your local police department and ask if they will send out a member of the cyber patrol team from their department. These people have tons of experience, information and tips for safety. Be careful, however, not to let them scare your audience. Remember, they primarily deal with Internet crimes, so their perspective might be a bit skewed.

- Make a copy of the Key Terms page (pp. 149-151) for each person.

- Set up the Virtual Tour as described on pages 144-145.

- Invite several parents and teens who are Internet savvy to be a part of a panel discussion (p. 145).

- Make a copy of the Blogging and Chatroom Tips (p. 152) page for each person.

- Make a copy of the Parent Action List (p. 153) and Technology Tools for Computer Safety (p. 154) for each parent.

- Optional: Combine all the handouts for this event into a booklet to be given to each person or family.

Event Outline

Explain It

Share with families your goals for the event:

- Information and Awareness—If you leave here today asking more questions than you came in with, we will be happy. We believe parents should be aware of what is happening online and how it is impacting their kids. We can't give you all the answers for your family today, but we can sure help you ask the right questions.
- Understanding—Every now and then we get to see life through someone else's lenses. Parents, hopefully you will see your teenagers' world a bit clearer because of the time we spend together tonight, and teens, you will understand your parents' struggles just a bit more as well.
- Balance—Because parents often don't understand the cyber world, they respond in one of two opposite ways. They decide that computers and the Internet are evil and ban their children from ever going online, or they throw up their hands, allowing their kids to roam the virtual world with no supervision or restrictions. We think there is a better, more healthy place in the middle.
- Action—We hope that you will put the information you receive into practice. We want the cyber world to be a better place for teens because of something you learn, talk about or do as the result of tonight.
- Encouragement—When parents and kids work together and try to understand each other, the cyber world can become a positive, productive and even edifying place!

Let's begin by taking a quick overview of the use of technology in families. A communication gap between parents and teens has always existed. In many cases the Internet has widened the chasm. This generation is the first to grow up "plugged in." New access to the world, combined with the technological anxiety that many adults face, has turned the gap into a digital divide. Share with your families the statistics[1] in the sidebar.

PARENTS' PERSPECTIVE

87 percent say they have established rules for their kids' Internet use

54 percent feel they are limited in their ability to monitor and shelter their kids from inappropriate material on the Internet

69 percent feel they know a lot about what their kids do on the Internet

31 percent have disciplined their child because of their Internet use

STUDENTS' PERSPECTIVE

36 percent say parents or guardians have NOT made rules for their use of the Internet

41 percent do NOT share what they do and where they go on the Internet with their parents

29 percent say their parent or guardian would disapprove if they knew what they were doing on the Internet

36 percent have NOT discussed how to be safe on the Internet with their parent or guardian

22 percent say the computer they use most often is in their room

73 percent say there is a need for kids and teens to learn about Internet safety

With these statistics in mind, at this event we are going to be talking specifically about freedom and boundaries as they relate to computer and Internet use. However, I think it is important for us to remember that determining your family's guidelines for computer use is just a small example of what is happening in your family on a much larger scale. The teen years can be one of the most exciting and challenging periods of the child-parent relationship. Your teen is beginning to mature physically, emotionally and intellectually and is anxious to experience increasing independence from parents. To some extent for parents this means loosening up on the reins, but by no means does it mean abandoning your parenting role. Teens are complicated in that they

demand both independence and guidance at the same time! As your family walks the tightrope of independence and guidance, we want to help you keep your balance online!

While this event is going to by nature focus on the negative side of Internet activity and its potential dangers, it is important to remember that most often kids are doing great things online. Share the statistics[2] in the sidebar.

86 percent of students use their computers to communicate with friends

85 percent use the computer for entertainment purposes

78 percent use the computer for general internet surfing

69 percent use the computer to work on homework

48 percent use the computer for reading and learning

48 percent use the computer to keep up with current events

Explain that these statistics show us that it is important to remember that the Internet can be an asset to our kids. And furthermore, with our world becoming more and more technology driven, computer and Internet skills can be vitally important skills for students to have. Distribute the Key Terms page to families and briefly review terms as necessary.

Computer Boundaries

Model It

Ask teens and parents what is happening online these days and what parents and teens need to talk about. Here is a sample list of topics and suggestions for a Virtual Tour of the Internet. Adapt the discussion and activities to fit the time and equipment you have available:

- Search Engines. Explain the logging on process and search engines. Show a few different search engine options (Yahoo, Google, MSN, etc.) and explain what they do. This is also a good time to talk about the filters that search engines offer. Do a few searches and take a look at what comes up.
- Surfing. After talking about search engines, take the time to surf the web. Ask families to call out subjects they want to learn about and look up a few things. Some parents will be surprised at how many positive resources are out there. You can visit your church's site, your family's web page and some of your other favorites.
- E-mail. Most people are probably familiar with e-mail, but going to an e-mail account might be fun for parents who are still stamp-lickers!
- MySpace. Use of MySpace is a highly debated activity. Many parents prohibit their children from being a part of this online community, while other parents allow it. You may feel it is best not to

make a value statement about MySpace but instead simply to explore and talk about the good and bad things that it contains. Show kids and parents how to protect themselves from some of the more negative things that happen in the world of MySpace.
- IMing. Kids are constantly IMing (instant messaging) each other and many parents don't understand what is happening. Converse with a friend online to give parents an idea of what this process is like.
- Chat Rooms. Chat rooms can be another hot button topic for parents. Explore a few different chat room options and jump into some conversations. During this process, talk about some of the dangers of talking to people online whom you don't know. Talk about how to protect yourself and what not to do.
- Blogging. Take families to a blog and do some reading and maybe even a little writing. It is fun to post something for others to read about your event. Maybe your church even has a place for members to blog about the worship services.
- Pornography. Pornography is an essential topic to be addressed. Pornography is the leading industry on the web and often this topic is one of parents' biggest fears. Obviously you aren't going to sign on to any inappropriate sites, but perhaps do a search on

"sex" and show the families how many sites are available. Then search for something innocent like "videos" or "pictures" and see how many porn sites are listed. This exploration will dramatically increase parents' awareness.

- History. Show parents where the computer records Internet history and how they can check the history of which websites have been accessed. Also talk about the ways kids delete history and what to look for when that is happening.
- ISP. Talk about where you get your Internet service from and how these places can help you with filtering
- Monitoring Websites. Show parents how they can register their computer for online monitoring through websites such as www.XXXChurch.com or www.CovenantEyes.com.
- Filtering and Monitoring Software. Many parents will be interested in how filtering and monitoring software works. Make sure the computer you are using has this software and show them how the software works.

Practice It

Ask a panel of teens and adults who are Internet savvy and willing to share their tips and ideas to sit in front of your group. Use the following questions to get things going and then invite parents and teens to ask questions.

- How do you spend your time on the Internet?

- What is your overall evaluation of the Internet? Is it good or bad? What are the plusses and minuses?
- What would you say to parents who leave their child's Internet use completely unsupervised?
- What would you say to parents who ban their child from Internet use?
- What are the plusses and minuses of MySpace?
- What are some of the tricks kids use to get around online rules and how can parents prevent them?
- What are some of teens' favorite online sites—good and bad?

After the panel discussion, give the following guidelines and tips:

- When you post anything online, remember that people are checking on you. Both college admissions officers and prospective employers do Web searches on people.
- Mistakes can last a long time online! What's uploaded to the Internet can be downloaded by anyone and passed around or posted online pretty much forever. Even if you delete things or change images, the old images are stored on other people's computers forever! And that's a long time!
- Be aware that people's (and students') inhibitions are often lower online. In other words you may do or say things online that you would never even consider in person.
- Be extremely careful when giving out personal information (see more on the next page).

The days when a child's home was a refuge from playground or neighborhood bullies is over. The Internet is the new playground, and there are no off hours. The popularity of instant messaging, e-mail, web pages and blogging means that playground bullies are on the prowl looking for targets all day, every day.

You do not have to accept any online activity that is meant to intimidate, threaten, tease or harm yourself or anyone else. Giving bullies attention is exactly what they want, so ignore them as much as possible. Never respond to e-mail, chat comments, IMs or other messages that are hostile, belligerent, inappropriate or in any way make you uncomfortable. Explain that if kids encounter a bully or any "weird" or "odd" comments, e-mail or posts online, they should:

- Tell a trusted adult.
- Never open, read or respond to messages from cyber bullies.
- Save messages from bullies. They may be needed to take action.
- Use software to block bullies if they encounter them through chat or IM.
- Tell their school if the bullying is school related or involves another student. All schools have bullying solutions.
- If you or your children are threatened with harm, contact your local police.

Distribute the Blogging and Chatroom Tips handout. As time permits, review and discuss the tips with parents and teens.

Summarize the information in this event with tips for parents and teens.

Tips for Parents

Don't be naive. Even kids with no Internet service at home are affected by access in school, libraries and friend's homes. Filters don't always work and kids are good at finding ways around the rules!

Don't be afraid. The Internet is an extremely useful tool that, like it or not, is a huge part of our world today. It can't be dismissed because it is sometimes confusing. The Internet can be an excellent way for you and your children to bond and share a common interest.

Don't overreact. Overreaction shuts down communication, and communication is perhaps the best protection you have. If your teen confides in you or is caught doing something inappropriate online, don't freak out. Try to work with your teen to prevent this from happening in the future. Remember, your teen will soon be an adult and needs to know how to exercise judgment in reaching his or her own conclusions on how to explore the Internet.

Get your kids to educate you. It's human nature to fear the unknown, right? So get some information about your child's online life directly from the source. Have your kid(s) show you around a bit. Take the tour of their online world.

Keep your computer in an open area. Location, location, location is not just a key term in real estate. Set up the computer in the kitchen or family room, so you can keep an eye on where your kids are going online and what they are doing. Don't allow kids to keep an Internet computer in their room! Be wary of webcams, especially located in teenager's rooms.

Check up from time to time. If you are concerned that your child is engaging in risky online behavior behind your back, you can do some detective work. Review the computer's history or use monitoring software to see where they've been. I suggest being upfront about this with your teens. Tell them you are going to be checking up on them from time to time so they don't feel betrayed when you do. An easy way to confirm your child's safe behavior online is to do a search by their name, nickname, friend's names, school, hobbies, grade or area where you live.

Checking up on your child's online behavior is not an invasion of their privacy if strangers can see it. There is a difference between reading their paper diary that is tucked away in their sock drawer and reading their MySpace. One is between them and the paper it's written on. The other is between them and 700 million people online!

Establish ground rules. Determine and communicate rules for your kids concerning computer use. Make sure

they know what is and what is NOT acceptable. Include these items in your rules: computer location, what info they give out, who they can interact with, sites they can and can not visit, when they can and can't be on the computer or Internet.

Above all, remember who's the boss! Surprise, it's not Tony or Angela! Repeat after me: "I'm still the parent!" If they don't listen or follow the rules, there will be consequences.

Tips for Teens

Don't overreact. Overreaction shuts down communication, and communication is foundational for trust. So communicate with your parents and you will build trust that leads to more independence through your teenage years.

Communicate with Mom and Dad. Talk with your parents about their expectations and ground rules for going online.

Educate your parents. An informed parent is a more relaxed parent. It's human nature to fear the unknown. So, because parents are human too, it's much more effective to explain what is happening online to your parents and show them around a bit than to just react by saying they're being absurd about your online activities.

Your parents are constantly exposed to newspaper articles and TV news shows about scary things happening online. A lot of parents don't know these examples aren't what normally takes place. You can help them get some perspective by telling them what your experience actually is and showing them around. Help your parents become advocates for safe, constructive Internet use. Make them part of the solution rather than part of the problem.

Be aware. Know that there are dangers on the Internet. Don't meet people offline that you met online! Don't post anything your parents, principal or a predator couldn't see. What you post online stays online—forever!

Be who you are. Don't do or say anything online you wouldn't say offline.

Take It Home

Give parents the Parent Action List. Ask your parents to place a check next to the following statements they will commit to. Distribute the Technology Tools

for Safety handout to parents so that they will have information about ways to filter or block inappropriate online activity.

Suggested Resources

The following are websites that provide additional computer safety guidelines and tips: Isafe.org, Staysafe.org, Safeteens.com, Blogsafety.com, Cybertipline.com, Netsmartz.org, Wiredsafety.org.

Find additional resources at www.faithbeginsathome.com.

Notes

1. 2003-05 i-SAFE survey of 4,500 parents. www.isafe.org (Accessed September, 2007.)

2. University of Kentucky, College of Agriculture, Youth Internet Usage statistics provided by Insight Express, August, 2004.

Network

Any time you connect two or more computers together so that they can share resources, you have a computer network. Connect two or more networks together and you have an internet.

internet (lower case i)

Any time you connect two or more networks together, you have an internet (as in inter-national or inter-state).

Internet (Upper case I)

The vast collection of inter-connected networks that are connected using the TCP/IP protocols that evolved from the ARPANET of the late 60s and early 70s. The Internet connects tens of thousands of independent networks into a vast global internet and is probably the largest Wide Area Network in the world.

Firewall

A combination of hardware and software that separates a network into two or more parts for security purposes.

ISP (Internet Service Provider)

An institution that provides access to the Internet in some form, usually for money.

Blog (weB LOG)

A blog is basically a journal that is available on the web. The activity of updating a blog is "blogging" and someone who keeps a blog is a "blogger." Blogs are typically updated daily using software that allows people with little or no technical background to update and maintain the blog.

Cookie

The most common meaning of "Cookie" on the Internet refers to a piece of information sent by a Web Server to a Web Browser that the Browser software is expected to save and to send back to the Server whenever the browser makes additional requests from the Server. Cookies might contain information such as login or registration information, online "shopping cart" information, user preferences, etc.

Cyberspace

Term originated by author William Gibson in his novel *Neuromancer*. The word "cyberspace" is currently used to describe the whole range of information resources available through computer networks.

Domain Name

The unique name that identifies an Internet site. Domain Names always have two or more parts, separated by dots. The part on the left is the most specific, and the part on the right is the most general. A given machine may have more than one domain name but a given domain name points to only one machine.

For example, the domain names matisse.net, mail.matisse.net and workshop.matisse.net can all refer to the same machine, but each domain name can refer to no more than one machine.

Download

Transferring data (usually a file) from another computer to the computer you are using. The opposite of upload.

E-mail (Electronic Mail)

Messages, usually text, sent from one person to another via computer. E-mail can also be sent automatically to a large number of addresses.

Search Engine

A system (usually web-based) for searching the information available on the Web. Some search engines work by automatically searching the contents of other systems and creating a database of the results. Other search engines contains only material manually approved for inclusion in a database, and some combine the two approaches.

Spam (or Spamming)

An inappropriate attempt to use a mailing list, or USENET or other networked communications facility as if it was a broadcast medium (which it is not) by sending the same message to a large number of people who didn't ask for it. The term probably comes from a famous Monty Python skit which featured the word spam repeated over and over. The term may also have come from someone's low opinion of the food product with the same name, which is generally perceived as a generic content-free waste of resources.

Spyware

A somewhat vague term generally referring to software that is secretly installed on a user's computer and that monitors use of the computer in some way without the user's knowledge or consent. Most spyware tries to get the user to view advertising and/or particular web pages. Some spyware also sends information about the user to another machine over the Internet. Spyware is usually installed without a user's knowledge as part of the installation of other software, especially software such as music sharing software obtained via download.

URI (Uniform Resource Identifier)

An address for a resource available on the Internet. The first part of a URI is called the "scheme." The most well known scheme is http, but there are many others. Each

URI scheme has its own format for how a URI should appear. Here are examples of URIs using the http, telnet, and news schemes:

http://www.matisse.net/files/glossary.html

telnet://well.sf.ca.us

news:new.newusers.questions

URL (Uniform Resource Locator)

The term URL is basically synonymous with URI. URI has replaced URL in technical specifications.

Virus

A chunk of computer programming code that makes copies of itself without any conscious human intervention. Some viruses do more than simply replicate themselves, they might display messages, install other software or files, delete software of files, etc. A virus requires the presence of some other program to replicate itself. Typically viruses spread by attaching themselves to programs and in some cases files, for example the file formats for Microsoft word processor and spreadsheet programs allow the inclusion of programs called "macros" which can in some cases be a breeding ground for viruses.

Web

Short for "World Wide Web."

Web Page

A document designed for viewing in a web browser. Typically written in HTML. A website is made of one or more web pages.

Website

The entire collection of web pages and other information (such as images, sound, and video files, etc.) that are made available through what appears to users as a single web server. Typically all the of pages in a web site share the same basic URL, for example the following URLs are all for pages within the same website:

http://www.baytherapy.com/

http://www.baytherapy.com/whatis/

http://www.baytherapy.com/teenagers/

The term has a somewhat informal nature since a large organization might have separate "websites" for each division, but someone might talk informally about the organization's "website" when speaking of all of them.

GENERAL TIPS

1. Be as anonymous as possible. Avoid postings that could enable a stranger to locate you. Information that should never be posted includes your last name, the name of your school, sports teams, the town you live in, and where you hang out.

2. Protect your personal information. Check to see if your service has a "friends" list that allows you to control who can visit your profile or blog. If so, allow only people you know and trust. If you don't use privacy features, anyone can see your info, including people with bad intentions.

3. Never arrange an in-person meeting. No matter how safe you think you are, the risk is too great.

4. Think before posting photos. Avoid posting photos that allow people to identify you (for example, when they're searching for your high school). Remember that sexually suggestive images will attract trouble! Before uploading a photo, think about how you'd feel if a parent, grandparent, college admissions counselor, or future employer saw it.

5. Check comments regularly. If you allow others to comment on your profile or blog, check them often. Don't respond to mean or embarrassing comments. Delete them and, if possible, block offensive people from commenting further.

6. Be honest about your age. Membership rules are there to protect people. If you are too young to sign up, do not attempt to lie about your age. Talk with your parents about alternative sites that may be appropriate for you.

People you meet in cyberspace might not be who they seem to be.

IDENTITY TIPS

1. Never give out your full name, address or phone number.

2. Don't post pictures that allow people to know where you live or go to school.

3. Never share your passwords or pin numbers.

4. Don't give out your social security number.

5. Don't post any information that identifies you or places you geographically.

I will . . .

☐ Move the Internet computer out of my child's room into a common area of our home.

☐ Take computers in kids' rooms offline.

☐ Establish Internet filtering on our home computer(s).

☐ Have my kids show me around their Internet world.

☐ Establish some rules and guidelines for our family's Internet use.

☐ Have a discussion with my kid(s) about Internet safety.

☐ Go over the Teen Tips with my child.

☐ Set an example through my appropriate use of the Internet.

☐ Continue to live in denial about what might be happening in the cyber world!

Even the best technology can only serve as a tool to supplement the primary job parents have of building character and virtues in their children. Our greater goal as parents is to help our children develop an "internal filter" to guide them when they leave the home.

There are three basic approaches to using technology to help your kids navigate the cyber world appropriately:

I. Filtering/Blocking Through Your ISP

Many Internet service providers (ISPs) now offer content filtering with your monthly service or for a small fee. This may be a better solution for your family than buying and installing filtering software. ISP filtering is activated at your ISPs office and content that isn't acceptable isn't transferred to your computer. Filtering software that is installed on your computer has the content transferred to your computer and then it is blocked. Some ISPs even offer filtering software that you can install. Either way, if you can get Internet filtering that is acceptable to your family with the service that you are already paying for, it worth checking out.

Advantages:
Blocks the material before it gets to your computer.

The cost may be included with the fee your already pay. Several filtering software packages require you to pay for updates after one year, so you could really save.

Instead of installing software, all you may have to do is call your ISP to activate the filtering or activate it online.

Most filtering software programs need to be updated and since your ISP will be updating the software, it won't be necessary for you to be concerned about the constant updating.

The filtering is much harder to override because the offending content isn't even delivered to your computer.

Disadvantages:
You may not be able to override the filtering if you want to view the site that is being blocked.

The content that is filtered may not coincide with your family's values.

If the ISP just provides software, you will still have to update it.

If you can activate the filtering online and your child has your password, the child can easily turn it off.

To see if your ISP offers filtering or parental controls, go to their homepage or give them a call.

2. Filtering/Blocking Through a Search Engine

Most major search engines get their listings by crawling the web. This means it's easy for possibly objectionable material to appear in search results. As a solution, most major search engines offer some type of filtering ability. It's meant to keep out material that most might not want children to encounter.

Advantages:
Blocks the material before it gets to your computer.

No cost.

No software or calls.

No updates needed.

Easy to bypass if you need to.

Helps with accidents.

Disadvantages:
Teens can get around this easily by using a different search engine.

Teens may be able to turn off the filter.

The content that is filtered may not coincide with your family's values.

Won't prevent teens looking for inappropriate material.

3. Filtering/Blocking/Monitoring Through Software on Your Home Computer

Filtering software works across the entire web, not just for search results. Most filtering software provides a fair amount of control for parents to determine what is and is not allowable content. The main advantage filtering software offers is that it tends to make it harder to access adult material on the Internet, although some of the applications available have other really useful features as well (restricting access to the computer to certain times, etc.). All filtering software works with one or a combination of the following three methods:

WHITE LISTS

Advantages:

This is the most useful of the filtering software applications provided for children. A White List is a list of "safe" sites—sites that are thoroughly checked and deemed safe for the majority of the population to view. These sites should never have any adult material of any kind on them and generally consist of entertainment and education related sites.

Disadvantages:

The disadvantage of White Lists is that the range of content accessible is severely limited. They are definitely useful, as children can safely plunder the approved sites, but the types of sites are so restricted that users miss out on a lot of the interesting and informative content that makes the Internet so popular. It also helps to know that the filtering software companies are not guaranteed to be impartial, and have been known to allow access to certain companies while restricting access to others that provide similar content.

BLACK LISTS

Advantages:

Black Lists are the exact opposite of White Lists. They prevent access to a list of sites that contain content that is not deemed appropriate by the creator of the list. These lists are usually well maintained (often weekly, although this varies) with adult content or themes that have been discovered by the maintainers of the filtering software regularly being added. Each software package generally keeps their black list secret (so their competitors can't use them) so there can be any number of sites blocked. Also, most software packages categorize their blocked sites under common themes, so you can choose which type of content you wish to block.

Disadvantages:

Black Lists are very popular, but for the purposes of safeguarding children are unfortunately close to useless. There are many ways to get around them, and the Internet is so vast and develops so rapidly that there is no guaranteed way to block all of the adult material available. These days Black Lists are generally used in combination with keyword filtering (see below), with well-known offensive sites banned by default.

KEYWORD FILTERING

Advantages:

Software that uses keyword filtering reads each page as it is downloaded and searches for a list of key words that the software maintainers have banned. Some programs will not display a page that contains any of the key words, and some programs just strip the word from the page. The major advantage to keyword filtering is that it can scan any site as needed, not relying on lists of sites compiled by the filtering software developers.

Disadvantages:
Sadly, the disadvantages of this technique are many. There is no way for the software to understand the context of a word, so many sites are blocked although their content is not actually offensive. For example, one software package blocks sites that use such words as "blonde," "explosive," "barely" and "amateur." These do regularly appear on adult sites, but there are far more that use these words in a neutral manner.

MONITORING

In addition to filtering and blocking, software can also help parents by monitoring. In other words, through the software parents will have access to a comprehensive unalterable history of all sites visited on the computer.

Advantages:
The advantages of this are quite simple. If you don't like the restrictions of filters and need more freedom on the Internet, monitoring allows full access to all websites. If inappropriate sites are visited, they will show up on the history and disciplinary action and correction can be taken. This system also provides accountability for parents using the Internet in the home.

Disadvantages:
The disadvantage of this system is that, by itself, monitoring does not filter out or block inappropriate sites or material. Accidents can occur and monitoring will not prevent this. Monitoring is a reactive system of accountability, not a proactive or prevention. It is however important to point out that monitoring can be used in combination with any of the above filtering/blocking tools.

EXAMPLES OF SOFTWARE

Cyber Patrol

Cybersitter

Kidsafe Explorer

MommaBear

NetNanny

We-Blocker

WebGuardian

Faith Mentoring— Establishing Another Voice

Target Age of Children

Teenagers

Goal of Take It Home Event

To help teenagers identify and establish an adult faith mentor they can turn to for advice and support, and to build a stronger relationship between the youth and adults of your congregation.

Note: This Take It Home Event has three parts. Part one will be a one-hour Mentor Orientation. Part two is a six-week Faith Mentoring Program where the student and mentor worship together and then go through the discussion guide together either before or after the service. Part three is a one-hour Mentor Wrap worship service.

Preparing for the Event

- Involve the senior pastor and leadership of the church in the planning process for this event to ensure that they will understand and support the Faith Mentoring Program you will be initiating. This event requires significant coordination and planning. Finding the right leadership is critical for the success of the Faith Mentoring Program.
- Determine what grades or ages of children will participate in the event.
- Establish the dates for each part of the event: Mentor Orientation (one week before the Faith Mentoring Program begins); Faith Mentoring Program (six weekend or midweek sessions); Mentor Wrap worship service (sometime during the week following the completion of the six-week Faith Mentoring Program).

- Ask parents to participate in the Mentor Orientation and the Mentor Wrap.
- Have students contact a mentor three to four weeks before the Mentor Orientation. (Optional: Provide a sample of "Will You Be My Mentor?" letter for students to use.) Each student is asked to find someone who will serve as a faith mentor for six weeks. The faith mentor must be an active member of the church, at least 35 years in age, not related to them, be a good example of Christian living and a person with whom the student will feel comfortable having a guided discussion of faith and life issues. Assign someone to track the students' progress to see how many are finding their mentors and how many will need mentors assigned to them at the Mentor Orientation. Anticipate that about 60 to 80 percent of your students will find their own mentor. For those students who don't know someone to ask to be their adult faith mentor, you will need to recruit adults who are willing to serve as mentors if needed. Print in your bulletin an announcement requesting mentor applications two to three weeks before the Mentor Orientation is held. All prospective mentors should be screened following your church's safety policy, and asked to attend the Mentor Orientation. They may not be needed, but you wouldn't want any student who wants a mentor

to go without one.
- Make copies of the Faith Mentoring Discussion Guides found on pages 162-167. Make at least one copy per student and mentor as well as some extras for those who forget theirs.

Mentor Orientation

The purpose of the Mentor Orientation is to get the Faith Mentoring Program off to a good start. Mentors, students and their parents are asked to attend the Mentor Orientation so all can have a clear understanding of how the program will work.

Mail a reminder letter to all mentors, students and their parents one week prior to the Mentor Orientation with the date, time and location of the orientation.

Mentor Orientation Schedule

PURPOSE: Explain the purpose of your Faith Mentoring Program (i.e. to establish another voice that will help nurture a student's relationship to God and to build bridges between the youth and adults of the congregation).

PLAN: Explain that mentors and students are to attend a worship service together and then complete a discussion guide together each week. The guide will take 20 to 30 minutes to complete. Give them time to discuss and determine the following things:

- What worship service will they attend?
- Where will they meet?

- When and where will they go through the discussion guides?
- When done, where will the parents reconnect with their son or daughter?

PRECAUTIONS: Present the following mentoring guidelines:

- Transportation of the child to and from meetings is the parent's responsibility. The parents must approve any transportation of the student by the mentor.
- If you cannot make the meeting due to unforeseen circumstances, be sure to notify your mentor or student. Exchange phone numbers.
- Never meet one-on-one with a youth in a private place. Always meet in a public setting (narthex, sanctuary, hallway, etc.).
- Keep all matters of discussion confidential, unless otherwise agreed. Confidentiality is an important ingredient of trust.
- Remember: It's OK not to have all the answers for each other. Allow the opportunity to ask questions of each other. Don't keep the conversation one-sided.
- Don't be afraid of silence during your discussions.

PREPARATION: Hand out the Faith Mentoring Discussion guides. Discuss the material in the guide and explain how the program will work. Both the mentor and student are to answer each question.

PRACTICE: Have the mentor, student and their parents discuss the following questions as a "warm up" for the upcoming six weeks.

- Where were you living at age five?
- What was or is your favorite and least favorite subject in school?
- If your house was burning and everyone was safe and you only had time to take three things out, what would you take?

Faith Mentoring Program

Each week of the six-week Faith Mentoring Program distribute the appropriate discussion guide. The discussion guides are designed to stimulate discussion and build a relationship between a teenager and an adult faith mentor. The theme verse is John 3:16: "For God so loved the world that he gave his one and only Son, that whoever believes in him shall not perish but have eternal life."

Mentor Wrap Worship Service

The Mentor Wrap Worship Service is the concluding event of the Faith Mentoring Program. Mentors, students and their parents are asked to attend this event that provides an opportunity for parents to reengage with some of the experiences that happened over the past six weeks. The service is also a time to make plans for ongoing opportunities and closure. On the next page is a sample Mentor Wrap Worship Service agenda.

10 minutes: **Time of Worship**

15 minutes: **Sharing Exercise (mentor and student share while parents listen)**

Answer the following questions:

- When we first got together, I remember thinking . . .
- One of the most interesting things I learned about you is . . .
- A way you have helped me is . . .
- The thing I like most about you is . . .

After providing enough time for everyone to answer the questions, invite people to share answers with the entire group. Have some prizes (dollar bills, coffee cards, candy bars, etc.) for people who share.

5 minutes: **Ongoing Opportunity**

Some of you may be asking, "What if we don't want to quit meeting together?" Go through some resources they can use if they choose to continue to meet together on some sort of regular basis.

10 minutes: **Pastoral Message**

10 minutes: **Thanksgiving Offering**

Hand out an index card to each mentor, student and as a worship song is being sung, have them complete on the card the following sentence starters:

- A Christ-like quality I see in you is . . .

- I'm thankful God brought us together because . . .
- My prayer for you is . . .

Once everyone has completed a card and the song is done, have the students and mentors exchange the cards with one another as their offering to each other.

5 minutes: **Closing Prayer and Sending Song**

Take It Home Resource

A good resource to provide for the students is *The Youth Bible* by Word Publishing. *The Youth Bible* has a variety of topics including anger, depression, doubt, drugs and alcohol, friends, judging others and peer pressure that you can explore. Each topic has a variety of Scripture texts to examine and personal stories and illustrations written by teenagers.

Suggested Resources

Burns, Jim. *The Word on Prayer and the Devotional Life.* Ventura, CA: Gospel Light, 2000.

Find additional resources at www.faithbeginsathome.com.

Week 1: Getting to Know God

Opening Prayer: Dear God, we ask that You would bless us as our mentoring relationship begins. Please bless the time that we have together, and give us courage to speak openly and honestly with one another and to learn from one another. In Your name, Lord Jesus, we pray. Amen.

1. Read the theme verse, John 3:16.
2. What is the most difficult thing that you have done or tried to do?
3. If you had to tell someone who God is, would that be easy or difficult? Why?
4. List seven things that complete the statement "God is . . ."
5. Complete this sentence: "A reason I know God exists is . . ."
6. How close do you feel to God in your everyday life?
   a. "I feel closer to God when . . ."
   b. "Sometimes I feel God is far away when . . ."
7. If you could ask God one question, what would it be?

Closing Prayer. Share your highs and lows from the past week. Close by praying for each other.

Week 2: Getting to Know the World

Opening Prayer: Dear Lord, we thank You for the world in which we live. Please forgive us for the way we mistreat our world, and help us to bring about Your kingdom in all we do. In Jesus' name, we pray. Amen.

1. Read the theme verse, John 3:16.
2. If you could go anywhere in the world, where would you go?
3. If a reporter from another planet were to come to you and ask, "What is the greatest thing that has happened or is happening on your world?" what would your answer be?
4. How is the world different today from the way it was:
    a. 25 years ago?
    b. 100 years ago?
    c. 2,000 years ago, when Jesus was on the earth?
5. What are some of the changes that are good? What are some of the changes that aren't so good?
6. What do you imagine God thinks about our world today? What things would God like? What things would God not like?
7. What will be different in our world 25, 100 and 2,000 years from now?
8. What do you see happening with Christianity in the future? What's our role in keeping the Christian faith alive for the future?

Closing Prayer: Share your highs and lows from the past week. Close by praying for each other.

Week 3: One and Only

Opening Prayer: Dear God, we thank You for sending Your one and only Son to die for us. Help us to never forget what You did for us. In Your name, Lord Jesus, we pray. Amen.

1. Read the theme verse, John 3:16.
2. How many children are in your family? How many in your mother's and father's families?
3. If you have brothers or sisters, describe your relationship with them. If you don't have siblings, describe your relationship with your best friend.
4. What are some good things about being a son or daughter? What are some difficult things?
5. What do you think were some good things for Jesus as the Son of God? What would have been some potentially difficult things?
6. If something tragic were to happen to you or to one of your family members, how would you feel?
7. How do you think God felt when He watched His one and only Son be crucified? Why did God let this happen?

Closing Prayer: Share your highs and lows from the past week. Close by praying for each other.

Week 4: Believe Me!

Opening Prayer: Dear Lord, You've given us many reasons to believe in You. Please help us to believe and obey You in all areas of our lives. In Your name, we pray. Amen.

1. Read the theme verse, John 3:16.
2. How would you define the word "believe"?
3. Complete this sentence: "Some things I believe in are . . ."
4. Now complete this sentence: "Some things I don't believe in are . . ."
5. How would you complete this statement? "Some things I used to believe in but no longer do are . . ."
6. Who are the people you believe when they tell you something? Why do you believe them?
7. If you wanted someone to believe you, how would you do it?
8. If someone were to ask you, "Do you believe in God?" how would you respond?
9. What has God done to make it easier for people to believe in Him?
10. In what ways is God still doing things today to help people believe in Him?

Closing Prayer: Share your highs and lows from the past week. Close by praying for each other.

Week 5: Death Changes Things

Opening Prayer: God, we know that in all things You work for good and that even in death we who believe in the death and resurrection of Jesus have life. Please help us to handle death as it surrounds us and to help those who have been affected by the death of loved ones. In Your name, Lord Jesus, we pray. Amen.

1. Recite the theme verse, John 3:16, from memory.
2. Have you (or someone you know) ever had an experience in which you thought you might die?
3. How did this experience change or affect you?
4. If you had one week to live, what would you do? Why?
5. What prevents you from doing those things today?
6. Have you ever lost a loved one or someone you were close to? How did this make you feel?
7. The theme verse says, "Whoever believes in him shall not perish." What does that mean? How does this change your outlook on life and death?

Closing Prayer: Share your highs and lows from the past week. Close by praying for each other.

Week 6: Life Everlasting!

Opening Prayer: Dear God, we thank You for the time we've had to get to know one another these past six weeks. Please continue to draw us closer to You and to each other in the days, weeks and years ahead. In Your name, Jesus, we pray. Amen.

1. Recite the theme verse, John 3:16, from memory.
2. What is the best Christmas or birthday gift that you've ever received?
3. If you could ask for any gift this year for Christmas, what would it be?
4. What do you think heaven is like? What does it look like? Who's there?
5. Do people your age think that the gift of heaven is better than any gift we could receive here on Earth? Why or why not?
6. If the person sitting across from you were to give you the gift you wanted in question 3, how would you respond? If the person sitting across from you were willing to give that same gift to someone else, to whom would you want that gift to be given?
7. Anyone who believes in Jesus Christ receives the free gift of eternal life. What do you think this means? How do you respond to this?
8. That gift is also available to anyone you know. Who are you telling about this free gift?
9. Who is someone you know who currently isn't a Christian but who you wish would become a Christian?
10. What can you do (or have you done) to help him or her know the love of Jesus Christ?

Closing Prayer: Share your highs and lows from the past week. Close by praying for each other.

Talking About
Dating, Kissing, Sex & Stuff

Target Age of Children

Teenagers

Goal of Take It Home Event

To engage teens on their level, challenging them to think through their sexual choices from a Christian worldview, and to bridge the gap between teens and their parents, effectively bringing Mom and Dad into the discussion.

Preparation for the Event

- Determine if you want to target a specific age or offer this event to all of your teenagers. Read the description of the two approaches (see p. 169) and decide which approach will work best in your church.

APPROACH 1—TARGET A SPECIFIC GRADE LEVEL

The preferable option is to target students in a specific grade. This would mean, for example, that your event would be open only to eighth graders and their families.

One advantage of this approach is the opportunity it provides to develop and grow your event year after year without having to overhaul or change the content. This allows you to spend less energy on what you are presenting and focus more on the emotional and relational dynamics of the kids in your group. For the most part, you will be able to repeat what you are doing each year with a new group of students, and the pitfalls of running a new program work themselves out over time and the quality of the event will improve.

An option for a smaller church that may not have many kids in each grade would be to offer this every other year and combine two grades.

Another reason for focusing the event on one grade level is the relational opportunity it presents. Not only will you bond with a specific subset of kids (i.e. just you and your freshmen), but the students in that grade level will also connect with each other as a class.

APPROACH 2—TARGET A RANGE OF GRADE LEVELS

The second option is to offer this event to a range of students (i.e., high schoolers, eighth to tenth graders, or underclassmen, etc.).

One advantage to this approach is that over a period of years your students and parents will be challenged several times to consider, reconsider and discuss the sexual challenges and choices teens and their families deal with.

Another advantage is the increased chance of a student connecting with this event at a critical time in their sexual decision-making history. Kids wrestle with sexual temptation at different times, and allowing students freedom in attending this event at the time most applicable for them can be very beneficial.

Another reason to consider this approach is simply critical mass. On some level, when talking with kids about an uncomfortable subject like sex, they will feel safe if there is a critical mass in the room. At times during this event you are going to want a smaller, more intimate atmosphere, but too small of a group may inhibit students, especially early in this event. If your individual classes of students are too small to achieve this critical mass, you may need to broaden your target audience.

- Take time to consider the following items to help you plan this Take It Home Event.

Maturity
As you decide who the event will be for, consider the maturity of your students. When are the majority of them starting to become aware, show interest in, and engage the opposite sex? Also consider that there is also a big difference in the maturity of your eighth graders in the spring as opposed to their maturity in the fall.

Mixing
If you are going to mix grade levels, consider the impact the older students will have on the younger and vice versa. This can be especially true if you are mixing middle schoolers (junior highers) with high school kids. Ask yourself, *Will the middle schoolers be intimidated or the high schoolers fail to take the event seriously if the other is present?*

Atmosphere
You are going to be discussing some very intimidating and personal topics with your students. Make sure you create an environment that increases the chances of your students opening up. Here are some tips for arranging the setting: Don't put more than one small discussion group in one room. Use spaces that fit the size of your group. Smaller spaces feel safer and more intimate.

Group Size
Again, make sure you have enough kids in one grade level for a critical mass.

Timing
Placing this event at just the right time on the calendar is an important consideration. You may want to consider planning this retreat during or before a time of increased sexual temptation for your students, e.g., in the spring just before your high school's prom since statistics show this is a night when many teens make poor sexual decisions.

- Plan the format of this Take It Home Event. This event is designed as an overnight retreat. The extended time is critical for teens as they process the information that will be presented. There are also many late-night, spontaneous, and very significant conversations that happen student-to-student and student-to-adult leader during an overnight experience. However, you may want to start with a one-day or evening experience to help your congregation feel comfortable, and then grow into an overnight retreat. Use the Schedule Options provided on the next page as a guide in planning your event.

Evening Schedule Option

4:00 p.m.	Session A (For Parents) What Are Kids Really Facing?
6:00 p.m.	Student Check-In (Pizza Dinner)
6:30 p.m.	Session 1 So Why Am I Here?
7:15 p.m.	Session 3 Is It Really Worth It?
8:45 p.m.	Session B (For Parents and Students) Let's Talk About Sex
9:30 p.m.	Dismissal

Retreat Schedule Option

Saturday

10 a.m.	Check-In
10:30 a.m.	Session 1 (Large Group) So Why Am I Here? Conflicting Messages
12:00 p.m.	Lunch (Session 1 Small Group During Lunch)
12:45 p.m.	Session 2 (Large Group or Age-Targeted Groups) Shades of Gray: I'm Not Having Sex, But . . .
2:45 p.m.	Fun Activity (Off-Site Activity Such as Bowling, etc.)
3:15–5:15 p.m.	Session A (For Parents) What Are Kids Really Facing?
5:30 p.m.	Dinner
6:30 p.m.	Session 3 Is It Really Worth It? Session 3 Small Group
8:15 p.m.	Evening Activities and Hang Out
10:00p.m.	Session 4 You Make the Call
11:00 p.m.	Kids and Leaders Go to Host Homes (Or Designated Overnight Place)

Sunday

8:00 a.m.	Session B (Parents Only) Let's Talk About Sex
8:45 a.m.	Session B (For Parents and Students)
9:30 a.m.	Dismissal

- Plan how you will promote this Take It Home Event so that you will get your students and parents there. Let me start this section by telling you what won't work: "Hey kids, we are going to help facilitate some deep conversation between you and your parents about sex. If that sounds like fun to you, please sign up and tell your parents to come, too." How will you get your kids excited about an event focused on sex when their parents are, on some level, going to be participating?
- First, you need to plan ways to promote the event to the kids. Here are some tips:

Raise Intrigue
Early on, put up signs reading, "DKSS is coming!" (without saying "Dating, Kissing, Sex & Stuff").

Build Suspense
Add in the words one by one, "Dating KSS is coming!"

Maintain Curiosity
When the word "Stuff" is revealed, ask the question, "What's the Stuff?" and tell students they will have to come to the weekend to find out!

Ignorance Is Bliss!
Don't highlight the parental involvement component for your kids. Don't lie or trick them, but since the parent time is a very small percentage of the weekend, focus on the other parts of the event with your kids.

Tell Them to Trust You
If your kids respond negatively to the idea of parents being a part of this event, promise you will not embarrass them!

- Second, determine how you will promote this event to parents. To maximize the impact of this event you MUST use the power of parental influence to get kids that wouldn't otherwise come. Most parents will be thrilled to hear you are going to discuss sex with their teen, and as a result will encourage their kids to attend. I recommend not only promoting this event to parents in the church bulletin and newsletter, but also sending a specific promotional letter home to parents (see p. 175) in which you speak personally about the importance of this event.
- Think through how you will encourage hesitant parents to be involved. A few parents will be tentative about sending their child to a retreat about sex, especially if it is coed and overnight. Parents have every right to question the content of this event, so be ready. Be open, honest and ready to give them details of what will happen. Have a schedule and materials ready for them to view ahead of time if they wish, and be very clear that the decision for their child to be a part of your event is THEIR CALL. Ultimately, you may be surprised at the relatively few parents who inquire about the

content ahead of time but there will be a few. Explain the schedule, what you are covering, how you are separating the boys and girls at different times and for the overnight and offer to let them view the video ahead of time if they wish.

Here is a letter received from a parent after one of the DKSS:

Dear Dave,

I had to write and let you know what a success the eighth-grade retreat was for our family. I have always tried to be very open about sex with Lisa (name changed) and told her the "facts of life" in third grade because I didn't want her learning it from her friends or through the school's health program. We have had a couple of discussions since. For example: what message some clothing and outward appearances may say to others, how silly some of her friends were starting to act around boys, "going out" with someone (what does that mean?) and when she has had a boyfriend and when they've broken up. But we never really got down to when to have sex. Not that I was avoiding it, but I didn't realize how close she was to it. Thank you for opening both of our eyes. We started talking in the chapel, continued in the parking lot and on our drive home, then changed clothes and left for her younger sister's concert still talking about it and continued through the parking lot at Armstrong (the local high school), where I'm sure the people walking behind us thought I'd lost my mind. Then, when we got home, I brought her dad into the conversation. (He had to take our younger daughter to her concert earlier and couldn't come to the meeting.)

We are so pleased with what was discussed and how she feels. Your very open and honest discussions have helped her to know that this may not always be easy and what to do before getting there! WOW! She knows that this is something that should be discussed before being done. She knows that if the boy RESPECTS her, he will wait. She knows all the consequences of having sex outside of marriage. I could go on and on. What you said reached her. I hope you continue to do this retreat as I have another daughter who will be in eighth grade in three years.

Thank you!

- Recruit reliable and trusted leaders to help you. Prepare them by providing them with as much information as possible up front. As with ANY youth event, there will undoubtedly be variations from the plan, but have a plan going in and adjust from there. Here are some things you may want to include in your leader packet: Leader Tips (pp. 178-179), event schedule, list of students and leaders, small group session materials (pp. 188 and 198).
- Plan how you will follow up after the event. Ever year following this event I send out a letter (p. 176) to all the students who committed to staying sexually pure until marriage. This letter not only reminds them of their commitment but also encourages them in their decision. Students who made commitments in subsequent years also get a letter (p. 177) encouraging and reminding them of their commitment. They will receive this letter annually until they are about 21 years old.

Session Outlines

The sessions that follow are meant to help you get started in putting together this Take It Home Event. Please use, alter, expand, combine, condense or even discard them to best fit the needs of your group.

Session 1: So Why Am I Here? Conflicting Messages

Session 1: Small Group

Session 2: Shades of Gray: I'm Not Having Sex, But . . .

Session 3: Sex Has a Price Tag (includes Survey)

Session 3: Small Group

Session 4: You Make the Call (includes Commitment Letters and Cards)

Parent Session A (For Parents)
What Are Kids Really Facing? (Includes Letter to Child)

Parent Session B (For Parents and Students)
Let's Talk About Sex (Includes Sex Has a Price Tag Video)

Dear Parents/Guardians,

Hi, my name is (your name). I am writing to give you some information about our upcoming Dating, Kissing, Sex & Stuff Retreat for (age level) to be held (date and time). As the name of our retreat suggests, the topic of discussion will be "Dating, Kissing, Sex & Stuff." As one student boldly asked me, "So what is the stuff?" And you may be wondering the same thing! Basically, our message to students on this retreat is that God created sex, it is a good thing, and God's plan is for sex to be experienced within the boundaries of a marriage relationship.

One of the highlights of our time together is a video message from Pam Stenzel, a renowned national speaker who has a captivating and powerful message. She talks primarily about the physical, emotional and spiritual consequences of sex outside the marriage relationship. I have heard many speakers on this topic, and Pam is by far the best. Parents will view this video during the Parent Time on (date). However, if you would like to preview Pam's message before it is shown to your son or daughter, or if you would like to talk with me in more detail about the contents of our retreat, I would love to talk. I invite you to please give me a call.

A small but important aspect of this event is the Parent Time. This is a mandatory part of the weekend, so please ensure that at least one parent/guardian per family attends. This is a time for parents to learn and discuss how to help and guide their kids through these difficult decisions. Session A (parents only) will be held (date, time, and place) and then Session B (parents and kids together) will be held at (date, time, and place). Coffee and doughnuts provided! The students will join us at (time) for a guided interactive discussion between parents and kids. We realize that sex can be an embarrassing topic for many students and their parents. So, while we want to encourage open discussion, we will do our best not to embarrass you! Our session will end at (time).

Enclosed you will find a letter from a parent participant (see sample on p. 173), a registration brochure and a Medical Release Form. Please return the registration and Medical Release Form by (date).

Thanks for being involved in this significant event. After more than (number) years of youth and family ministry, I believe this retreat is one of the best things we can do for our students. TOGETHER we can help our kids make informed, healthy, God-honoring sexual decisions.

Sincerely,

Dear

Thank you so much for being a part of this year's Dating, Kissing, Sex & Stuff retreat. It was a wonderful weekend and we all learned a lot. After such a great experience, I just wanted to take a second and write to tell you how proud of you I am! The decision you have made to remain sexually pure from this point forward until the day you are married is I believe one of the best choices a young person can make. This decision can and will affect the rest of your life in so many positive ways. You will be free from the risk and worry of disease and pregnancy, you will gain the confidence that comes with making the tough choice to respect yourself and one day you will have an amazing gift to give your spouse and children. But finally, and most importantly, I believe this is God's best for you, and as a result of following His plan you will experience the joy that only a life lived with and for Him can bring.

With that, I also know it isn't and won't be easy. You are going to experience pressure from friends, (boyfriends or girlfriends) and others that will tempt and test the commitment you've made. God, however, is faithful to His children and will be there to give you strength, courage, character and integrity when the going gets tough (see 1 Corinthians 10:12-13). Remember that you are not on this journey alone. God is always with you, hopefully your parents and friends are with you, and we at church are here to support you. If you ever need help with anything or even just someone to talk to, we want you to know that our doors are always open and we are here to help. Thanks again for your inspiration to me, your friends, this church and our entire community. You truly are the light of the world (see Matthew 5:13-16)!

In Him,

P.S. Enclosed is another copy of the Commitment Card that you signed on the DKSS weekend. If on the craziness of the weekend you lost your original, I want to encourage you to sign this one and keep it in a special place where it can remind you of your commitment.

Dear (name),

It has been quite some time since we were together on the Dating, Kissing, Sex & Stuff retreat and I know you are not the same person now that you were then. However, I still want to take a second to remind you of and encourage you in your decision to remain sexually pure until the day you are married. I still believe this is one of the best choices you have made and can continue to make. It is a decision that has and will affect the rest of your life in so many positive ways. You will be free from the risk and worry of disease and pregnancy, you will gain the confidence that comes with making the tough choice to respect yourself and one day you will have an amazing gift to give your spouse and children. Finally, and most importantly, I believe this is God's best for you and as a result of following His plan you will experience the joy that only a life lived with and for Him can bring.

With that, I also know it hasn't been and won't be easy. You will continue to experience pressure from friends, (boyfriends or girlfriends), and others that will tempt and test the commitment you've made. God, however, is faithful to His children and will be there to give you strength, courage, character and integrity when the going gets tough (see 1 Corinthians 10:12-13). Remember that you are not on this journey alone. God is always with you, hopefully your parents and friends are with you, and we here at church are always here for you. If you ever need help with anything or even just someone to talk to, we want you to know that our doors are always open and we are here to help. This is the case whether you have kept your commitment or not. Always know that our God is one of second, third and even fortieth chances. When it comes to God, it is NEVER too early or late to start making good sexual choices. If you have kept your commitment, great job, keep it going! If not, you can start again right now. Thanks again for your inspiration to me, this church and our entire world. You truly are the light of the world (see Matthew 5:13-16)!

In Him,

Our Goal

What is our goal this weekend? There are many ways to say it but, ultimately, we want God's best for these kids. We want them to follow God in their sexual choices. We want them to understand that God loves sex, created sex and has given us sexual boundaries for our protection and welfare. Sex has the power to be such a source of blessing in our lives if we use it God's way, and an equally destructive force if we abuse it. Our goal this weekend is to both steer these students away from the pain and destruction of abusing sex in the way our world would lead them to do, and also to help them commit to sexual purity as they anticipate the tremendous joys of God-given sexuality within the context of marriage!

Authenticity Wanted

Even if kids are sharing thoughts and opinions that you do not share or EVEN that God does not share, don't shut them down. We want these kids to be real. They will hear a CLEAR message of what God wants throughout the weekend in manageable doses at appropriate times!

Our Lines and Boundaries

It would be great if we could allow kids to draw their own lines and boundaries for sexual behavior based on their desires to glorify God and fully experience the blessings He has for them. The ideal attitude is, "How can I have relationships that glorify God?" but, unfortunately, some will have a "How much can I get away with?" approach. Kids sometimes need concrete rules and boundaries. They sometimes need us to help them determine right and wrong. So, after much discussion with parents, kids and youth staff, it is recommended that kids are called to go no further than kissing.

Let the Process Work

The weekend builds on itself and is a process to help THE KIDS make decisions for themselves. If we help them think through the issues instead of telling them the answers to the issues, their convictions will be much stronger and last longer. They will receive answers and boundaries. However, before we share our thoughts, we want kids to wrestle with these decisions themselves, so don't panic if kids aren't coming up with the boundaries you want right away.

Don't Dominate Conversation

People will listen if they are listened to. The same is even more true with students! They are going to be talked AT for about half of our session time together. The other session time and small groups are for them to talk. You are here to share your perspective, wisdom and experience, but make your comments concise and to the point. Don't ramble on and on. That's what I'm here for!!!

Have Fun!!!

We are talking all weekend about a GIFT we have been given by God—the gift of sex and sexuality. There will be serious times and intense conversations but when appropriate, laugh and have a good time. A joyful attitude about sex has been missing from Christ-following communities for too long.

Pray

Scripture tells us to pray continually. Instead of overwhelming the teens, pray constantly for (names of leaders), and most importantly for the KIDS. Pray that God uses this weekend to do a work in their heart!

Dating, Kissing, Sex & Stuff

Session 1: So Why Am I Here?

Goal of the Session

To help the kids feel comfortable, to gain credibility for yourself by showing them that you understand their world, and to help them accept and feel comfortable with the idea that they and their peers have varying levels of sexual experience.

Preparing for the Session

- Purchase the PowerPoint Game "Animal Sex." This game is part of *The Power of Sex: A 6-Week Super Series* by Doug Fields. Order this product online at simplyyouthministry.com.
- Photocopy a Getting Ready page (see p. 185) for each student.

Opening Ice Breaker

Start right in with the PowerPoint Game "Animal Sex." This game presents interesting trivia and facts about all kinds of animals having sex. Sound a little risqué? It is and it will shock your kids and help them feel more comfortable about the subject matter.

Explain It

Introduce the following ground rules for the event:

- Schmoopiness. Although the title of our weekend is DKSS, we will not actually be participating in dating, kissing, sex and stuff on the weekend. (Sorry if any of you are disappointed!) This rule means that if you are here with your boyfriend or girlfriend, you are not going to be able to kiss, cuddle or hold hands this weekend. Boys are blue, girls are pink and these colors won't mix to form PURPLE! Sorry!
- Maturity. Act like adults not third graders. Explain to your kids that this is a weekend filled with adult content. Explain that some of the material discussed may make them feel uncomfortable and how they react and respond to those feelings is what shows maturity. Tell them that they may be tempted to make jokes, laugh, giggle, or make inappropriate comments to relieve the uncomfortable tension or feelings they might have, but maturity is being able to deal with those feelings, understanding that they are natural and nor-

mal when discussing this subject matter. Challenge your students to step up their maturity and act like adults. They will respond!

- Confidentiality. This is a closed weekend in terms of sharing. As leaders we are going to respect anything you share with us this weekend by keeping it confidential, and we expect you to show the same respect to each other. What is shared in this community stays here! (This is the one and only way in which our retreat resembles Las Vegas.) Your ability to do this is another way you show respect for one another and personal maturity.

- Authenticity. Challenge your students to be REAL not just RIGHT. Ultimately, for the most part we all know the right answers this weekend, but that is not really what we are interested in. This is a safe environment for you to not just be right but be real. We want to hear and wrestle with what you really think, with the questions you really have, with the doubts you sometimes think and with behaviors you are engaged in or are maybe just considering. The more authentic you are this weekend, the more you will get out of it.

Getting Ready Activity

Hand out a Getting Ready page to each student and ask kids to spend the next few minutes thinking about and writing their answers to the questions on the page:

- Why are you here?
- What do you expect to learn?
- What are you hoping to learn?
- What are your current convictions about dating, kissing, sex and stuff?

Inspire Them

Tell several stories of your own adolescent experiences, or you might want to have three different leaders with different adolescent experiences share their stories. (Optional: Tell the following stories from Dave Teixeira.)

My First Kiss: It was the summer between my seventh and eighth grade when I got invited to Suzy's birthday party. There were five boys and five girls. After the cake, ice cream and a few traditional party games, we all headed down stairs to Suzy's basement where the plan was for us to watch a movie. Instead, with Suzy's parents safely upstairs and the basement door closed, a new idea was born. What ensued was a game that combined what are traditionally referred to as "Spin the Bottle" and "Two Minutes in Heaven." We sat in a circle boy-girl-boy-girl and took turns spinning the bottle that was placed in the center. If, on your spin, the bottle came to rest pointing towards a member of the opposite sex, the two of you had to get up and go into Sally's basement closet with the lights out and door shut for two minutes.

Well, it just so happened that sitting in the circle that afternoon was a girl named Kristen. My friend had heard from her friend, who had talked to another friend, who had talked to Kristen, who had told her, that she had a "crush" on me. So, on my turn, as the bottle spun around in the center of the circle, my only hope and prayer was that the bottle would not come to rest on Kristen! But, you know what happened. Almost as if it were a cruel joke, the bottle spun, slowed and came to a stop pointing directly at Kristen. So, into the closet we went. It was a walk-in closet with no windows, so it was pitch black. We walked in, stood facing each other, the door was closed and we were engulfed in total darkness.

Now, at this point in my life, I had a very limited experience with girls. I had never kissed or held hands with a girl, had never had a girlfriend and was for the most part terrified of girls in general. A ladies man I WAS NOT. But here I was, standing in a closet, in the dark, directly in front of a girl who I knew had a crush on me. To this day, it is still the scariest moment of my life. My hands were sweaty, my heart was racing and my mind was going a million miles an hour. With my brain working overtime, it took me only moments to formulate a plan. I would simply stand there perfectly still and say and do nothing for the entire two minutes. That was my plan.

Well, after about 30 seconds,

Kristen took matters into her own hands. Tired of waiting for me to "make the first move," Kristen leaned in and planted one on me. And I mean PLANTED. This was no innocent peck on the cheek or lip-lock. We are talking full on tonsil-cleaning tongue action. Kristen wasn't playin' around! When the countdown outside the room started, "10, 9, 8, 7, 6 . . ." Kristen backed off, the door was opened and we walked out.

And that my friends, is the story of my unintentional, unsuspecting, and somewhat unwilling first kiss.

Home Alone: So now that you have a feel for who I was in the eighth grade, let me tell you a little bit about my best friend. His name was Nate and he was much cooler than me. Nate had an older brother, who was himself a bit of a ladies man, and so unlike me, Nate was privy to a lot of insider information about girls. Plus, it probably didn't hurt that Nate didn't wear glasses with lenses the size of coasters either! Nate was going out with this girl named Deana, and as a result I started "seeing" her best friend Janine.

One afternoon Nate and I were just hanging out when we got a call from the girls. They were at Deana's house with her parents gone for the afternoon and so they suggested we should cruise over. So Nate and I jumped on our bikes and

182

headed that way. We arrived and sat around Deana's living room making some small talk and that awkward middle school "we're dating but we never really talk" lull in the conversation happened. Then, all of a sudden, Nate and Deana get up and go upstairs to her parent's bedroom. After about half an hour, Nate and Deana come down, we say goodbye, hit the bikes and start for home. On the way home Nate tells me about his time upstairs with Deana. He went "up her shirt," "down her pants," and she had given him a "hand job." In Nate's mind, he was striking the perfect balance. He was enjoying some erotic sexual experiences while retaining his virginity.

Hallway Buzz: I got off the bus that Monday morning and the buzz in the school hallway had already started. I went to a middle school with just seventh and eighth graders and about 100 kids per grade. Everybody knew everything and news traveled fast. James and Kelly were a hot couple in the eighth grade that year and had been dating for a while. James was a buddy of mine from the basketball team, and it turned out that over the weekend, while their parents were out of town, his older brother had thrown a party. Kelly had come over to that party, and the big news in the hallway that Monday morning was that Kelly and James had had sex! This was big, because for me, it was the

first time I remember hearing that someone my age had had sex. The story was confirmed that day after school in the locker room as James boasted about his conquest and received high fives from the guys. Not long after, Kelly and James broke up.

So why did we tell these stories? Some of you think this retreat isn't for you! You might belong to one of these groups:

Group 1: Some of you relate to ME! You've had none or very little experience with the opposite sex. You may or may not have had a boyfriend or girlfriend EVER. You may or may not be interested in boys or girls right now in your life.

However, here is why this retreat is exactly for you: It's not a matter of IF you are going to find yourself at a party, in a closet, on a date, in a car or whatever . . . and you are going to have sexual choices to make. That day will come and it may come sooner than you think! So this retreat is about you having the chance to think through your choices now, before you find yourself in a compromising situation. This retreat is for you!

Group 2: Some of you relate to my buddy Nate. You've dated a little. You've had some emotional and physical experience with the opposite sex. Maybe you have an older brother or sister who gives you information. You may have even had a variety of sexual experiences on various levels. BUT you're NOT having sex, so you don't really need a lecture.

Session 1: So Why Am I Here?

Here is why this retreat is exactly for you. DANGER! DANGER! You are walking down a fine line. You are engaging in activities that have more EMOTIONAL, SPIRITUAL, and even hormonal PHYSICAL power than you can even imagine. You think you are in control, but you are deceiving yourself. Have you thought through:

- What you're doing?
- Why you're doing it?
- Where it's going?
- The feelings involved?

This retreat is for you!

Group 3: Some of you may relate to my buddy James: you've already had sex. And some of you might be saying, "No, not in eighth or ninth or tenth grade" or "Why would a kid who is already having sex show his or her face here?" Well, maybe your parents made you come. Maybe you didn't really know what you were getting into today. Maybe deep down inside there is a still small voice that is telling you something isn't right and you decided to open your heart just a little bit and come today.

To you I want to say: THANK YOU! Thank you for having the courage to be in this room. You may think you have all the info, but you don't (and if you allow yourself to engage this weekend you may find out how little you really do know). You may feel like it's too late, but it's not!

Here is the awesome truth; we have a GOD who never gives up on us. We have a God that gives not just second, but third, fourth, tenth and one hundredth chances. This retreat is for you!

In fact, it is never too early, unneeded or too late to start making good sexual choices when it comes to God. It is never too early for inexperienced Daves. It is never unneeded for exploring and experimenting Nates. It is never too late for been-there-done-that James and Kellys.

No matter where you are on this spectrum, I believe God wants to impress His love, grace and truth on your heart today. Lead group in a prayer. After the prayer, move directly into Session 1—Conflicting Messages (p. 186-187).

Why are you here?

_____
_____
_____
_____
_____

What do you expect to learn?

_____
_____
_____
_____
_____

What are you hoping to learn?

_____
_____
_____
_____
_____

What are your current convictions about dating, kissing, sex and stuff?

_____
_____
_____
_____
_____
_____
_____
_____

Dating, Kissing, Sex & Stuff

Session 1: Conflicting Messages

Goal of the Session

To raise awareness in kids concerning the sexual messages the media is constantly feeding them, and to help them understand God's message about sex and see how His message has been distorted by the media.

Preparation for the Session

- Collect Bibles, whiteboard and marker.

Opening

Begin by asking students, "What are your favorite TV shows and movies?" As they call out the names, write them up on a whiteboard in front of the room.

Then ask, "What are the sexual messages of the movies and shows we have just listed?" Lead students to consider each movie or show and determine if there is a sexual message, and if so, what it is. Write messages on whiteboard (see p. 187).

The kids will discover that many of the movies and shows they watch do have a sexual message and that the message given is:

- It's fun.
- Everyone's doing it.
- If you are cool, you're doing it.
- There are no consequences.

Optional: Spice up the time by interspersing current, top-rated movie clips that reinforce what you are trying to show them.

Explain It

After establishing that much of what the media says about sex seems to portray a fun, free for all, fornicating lifestyle, ask, "What does God say about sex?" The kids will give answers such as "Don't do it," "It's bad," "It's for love only," "It's for marriage."

Accept student responses, writing them on the whiteboard also. Expand this time by having kids read some of the following Bible verses as part of the discussion.

- God created sex—Genesis 1:27; Genesis 2:18-25.
- God wants us to enjoy sex—Song of Songs 4:1-6; Song of Songs 5:10-16.
- God puts some boundaries around sex—Hebrews 13:4.

It is clear that God is not anti-sex. God created sex and He created it as pleasurable and enjoyable. However, God created sex with boundaries. Why?

Tell this illustration:

It is kind of like a fire on a cold winter day. You build a fire in your fireplace and it is cozy and warm, something very enjoyable. However, if you build that same enjoyable fire in the middle of your living room, it will go from being enjoyable to being very dangerous and extremely destructive. Sex is the same way. When it is used inside the boundaries it was created for, it is a wonderful thing. But, if used outside that boundary, it will be like that fire in the middle of your living room—destructive.

So what is God's boundary for sex? Read Hebrews 13:4 aloud. God uses sex within the marriage relationship for two main reasons:

- Procreation, making babies, having children;
- Intimacy and oneness, a connection between the couple.

When God warns us time and time again not to step outside the boundary He has given us for sex, it is not to ruin our lives and make us miserable. No, God gives us a boundary to protect us from damage, hurt and pain.

Later on we are going to talk about the reality of physical, emotional and spiritual consequences of having sex outside of the boundary of marriage, but for now let's just review.

Send the kids to their small groups for a time of sharing, processing Session 1 and getting ready for Session 2.

MEDIA	GOD
It's fun!!!	It's fun!!!
Everybody's doin' it!	Married people should do it!
No consequences!	Serious consequences.
If you're cool, you're doin' it!	If you're smart, you'll wait

Dating, Kissing, Sex & Stuff

Session 1: Small Group

Goal of the Small Group

To get kids feeling comfortable as they talk and share. (Session 2 will have more intense material that gets increasingly personal. This sharing time will help prepare them for that.)

Opening

Go around and have each member of the group share three things about themselves (not necessarily about a sexual topic). Two of the things should be true and one should be a lie. Then have the rest of the group try to guess which one is the lie.

Discussion

After completing the opening activity, ask, "How is this activity like the way sex is portrayed in the media?" (Some things are true and some are false.) Give some examples you have experienced.

Continue the discussion by asking the following questions:

- When was the first time you learned about sex? Where were you and who told you? What was your reaction?
- What TV shows and/or movies did you think of for the list we made together?
- What are these programs telling you about sex?
- What is one thing you were surprised to learn in our first session?
- Who or what do you think has the most influence on your friends' sexual choices? Why?

Dating, Kissing, Sex & Stuff

Session 2: Shades of Gray: I'm Not Having Sex, But . . .

Goal of the Session

To encourage conversation that enables kids to wrestle with what they believe about a number of sexual topics.

Preparation for the Session

- Become familiar with the topics and suggested questions in the Discussion Topics (pp. 190-194).
- Prepare to lead the session by reading over the Session Tips (see below) and the following ground rules for success: What's said in the group, STAYS in the group! Be real. Respect other's thoughts and questions.

SESSION TIPS

1. Prepare students by telling them they're about to talk about some heavy stuff. Encourage honesty and confidentiality. Let the kids know that you want them to express what they experience, how they really feel and the questions they want answered. As a leader, don't be too quick to share your thoughts or give the right answers.

2. Frequently ask students to explain why they think what they think. (This helps them really think through what they believe. Most of them have never done this!)

3. Allow them to dialogue with each other.

4. Ask follow-up questions such as, "What do the rest of you think about that?" or "Does anyone else think something different?"

5. Affirm students who share thoughts that differ from the rest of the group, even if they are off-base.

6. Don't talk for too long at any one point.

7. Assure them that the questions, thoughts and feelings they have are common and normal.

8. Don't be afraid to laugh when it is appropriate (not at the students, of course).

Opening

To get students talking, have each person tell his or her name, school, and one of the following:

- You have one minute to address the entire nation, what would you say?
- What is the weirdest dream you've ever had?
- If you had to teach a school subject, what would you teach and why?
- If you could have one super power, what would it be?

Discussion Topics

This segment of the session is kind of like a "choose your own adventure" as you use topics from the discussion list that fit your group. Use the questions and ideas to keep things moving along.

Dating

- At what age should a teenager be allowed to single date?
- Are you allowed to go on dates? If not, do you disagree?
- What age are you allowed to begin dating?
- What does a typical "date" look like to you? (Dinner, movie, kissing, etc.)
- Why do people go on dates?

If you date, why do you do it?

- What is the purpose or goal of dating as a teenager?
- Talk about single dating verses group dating. What are the pluses and minuses?
- Should Christian dating look different from a secular date? Why? Should Christians even date?

Sexual Boundaries

- How far is too far? (Refer to the progression at the bottom of the page.)
- Do you have sexual boundaries set for yourself? Why or why not?
- How far do you think someone should be allowed to go sexually before they are married? Why?
- What if one person has a different boundary than the other?
- Will "fooling around" lead to sex?
- What would you do if your boyfriend or girlfriend wanted to have sex with you?
- Let's pretend that your future (wife) is out there right now but you don't know (her)—you've never met. Let's say that (she) is the same age as you, in the same grade and tonight (she) is going on a date. How far do you want your future spouse to go with someone else before (she) marries you?

Hold hands   Kissing   Touch above the waist   Touch anywhere   Mutual masturbation   Oral sex   Sex

God's Best

As you think about dating, it's not a question of how far can you go or what you can get away with. It is a question of what God wants from and for you. What do you want for your husband or wife and marriage? What do you think is the purpose or goal of intimate physical interaction with another person?

Diminishing Returns

The first time you held hands it was super exciting. After a while, it just seemed normal. So then you start kissing and, WOW, it's exhilarating! After a while, that isn't very exciting anymore. This process of experiencing diminishing sexual excitement will lead you further and further down the road of sexual compromise and that is a slippery slope.

Slippery Slope

Do you know what's happening when you're engaged with another person in the ways we've been talking about? Your body is preparing for intercourse. Guys, that's what an erection is. An erection is preparation for intercourse. That is your body preparing to have sex. Gals, your body is lubricating when you are sexually involved. That is your body preparing for sexual intercourse This preparation is God's design! He has designed your body to get ready for sex—not to get ready and then suddenly stop.

Tell students this illustration:

In Yosemite National Park there is a giant rock mountain called "Half Dome." It is literally shaped like a giant dome cut in half. The unusual thing about Half Dome is that

hikers are always very cautious and worried about falling off the steep side of Half Dome which is the flat side that goes straight down. However, 99 percent of the accidents (even deaths) happen on the not-so-steep curved side of this mountain. This is because the danger on this side is very gradual, lulling the climbers into a state of security and safety. Then, before they know it they are falling, unable to stop themselves. The steep side represents sex. "Oh no! Don't fall in to that!" But the other side represents the "slippery slope" that SO MANY fall into slowly and gradually. You think you're safe. You feel secure, but before you know it you've gone too far!

It is very hard to work your way backwards. Just like in life, doing something the first time is always the most difficult, but after that, after the barrier has been broken or the line crossed, it just gets easier and easier to do and harder and harder to stop!

Some people may say that they and their future spouses will benefit from sexual experience. After all, doesn't practice make perfect? Don't I need to practice so I can perform well for my future husband or wife? No, sex works with everyone. There is a lie out there that says, "You have to try it out before you are married because you might not be 'sexually compatible.'" This is a LIE. Trust me, if you like and truly love someone you are compatible. It isn't rocket science, it is sex. IT WILL WORK!

Don't worry that you will draw the line too high. I've never heard a married couple say, "We wish we would have done more or gone further physically before we were married. It was such a drag on our relationship that all we did was kiss before we got married."

Have students read these Scriptures and ask them to tell what advice is found: 1 Corinthians 6:13-20, 1 Corinthians 14:20, Colossians 3:5, 1 Timothy 5:1-2, 2 Timothy 2:22, 1 Thessalonians 4:3-5.

Pornography

- What is pornography? Sexually explicit pictures, writing, or other material whose primary purpose is to cause sexual arousal.
- Where do we see pornography?
- Is pornography a problem in America? In your school? With your friends?
- Is pornography harmful to the viewer? How so?
- Can you become addicted to pornography?
- How does it affect the way we view women or men?
- What does the Bible say about pornography?

Bring a bag of candy. Pull out a bar and ask, "Is this anyone's favorite?" Pass out a few different bars this way. Then ask the kids to read the nutritional contents on the back of the wrappers. Ask, "Is candy good for us?" (No way.) "Then why do we eat it?" (Instant gratification.) "What happens to people who eat this kind of junk food over the long haul?" (It harms their bodies.) "If you eat this one candy bar, is your desire for candy fulfilled for a short time, a long time or forever?" (A short time. Soon you will desire more.)

Pornography is the same as candy. It is not good for you, it will destroy your life, and the more you consume the more you desire.

Have students read these Scriptures and ask them to tell what advice is found: Matthew 5:28, 1 Corinthians 6:13b, 1 Corinthians 6:18-20, Ephesians 5:3, 1 Thessalonians 4:3-5.

STATISTICS[1]

CHILDREN:

100,000 websites offer illegal child pornography

Child pornography generates $3 billion annually

90 percent of 8-16 year olds have viewed porn online (most while doing homework)

Average age of first internet exposure to pornography is 11 years old

Largest consumer of internet pornography 12-17 age group

ADULTS:

20 percent of men admit accessing pornography at work

13 percent of women admit accessing pornography at work

In one study, 53 percent of PromiseKeeper men viewed pornography the previous week

10 percent of adults admit having internet sexual addiction

Masturbation

- What is masturbation? Manual stimulation of the genital organs of yourself or another for sexual pleasure.
- When was the first time you heard about masturbation?
- Where were you and who told you?
- What was your reaction?
- Is it normal?
- Is masturbation harmful? Addictive?
- Is it a sin?
- What does the Bible say about masturbation? Why is it silent?

Have students take turns reading the following Scriptures and telling what advice is found: Matthew 5:28, 1 Corinthians 6:13, 1 Corinthians 6:18:-20, Ephesians 5:3,1 Thessalonians 4:3-5.

You may choose to explain the following two perspectives regarding masturbation. One perspective regards masturbation as a sin. "Ninety-eight percent of all masturbation involves lustful mental fantasies or pornography. Most all of it, then, is a sin. I say why quibble over *whether* to call masturbation a 'sin' when most of it clearly *is* a sin."[2]

A second perspective is that masturbation cannot be proved to be a sin. "Some of the arguments against Christians masturbating are that it might involve pornography, it might involve sinful fantasizing, it might decrease the desire for one's spouse, it might become addicting, and so on.

However, these arguments do not prove that masturbation is a sin. After all, masturbation can be done without any of those things happening. For example, driving a car might involve exceeding the speed limit or running a red light (both of which are wrong), but this doesn't mean that driving a car is wrong in itself. In a similar way, masturbation can involve certain things which are wrong, but this doesn't mean that masturbation itself is wrong. Masturbation can be done without any of the above things happening, so those arguments do not prove that masturbation itself is a sin."[3]

There are two primary things for students to understand about masturbation, especially the guys.

First, God does not hate you if you masturbate. You are not a gross, disgusting pervert if you masturbate. Masturbation is something most men wrestle with at some point in their lives. Never let masturbation separate you from approaching and having a relationship with God.

Second, masturbation can (and often does) lead to sinful actions: fantasies, pornographic images and addiction. Be very careful with what you look at, what you think about and how often you masturbate, if you do it at all.

Body Image (Primarily for Girls)

Ask girls to share something they like about themselves physically or something they wish they could change. Have some magazines for the girls to look through and as they browse through the pages, ask them to describe what a woman should look like.

- How does the media affect your body image?
- Why do we care so much about our looks?
- Does our "look" define us?
- What does God look at? (See 1 Samuel 16:7.)
- How are women who dress skimpy really viewed?

The barrage of messages about thinness, dieting and beauty tells "ordinary" women that they are always in need of adjustment—and that the female body is an object to be perfected.

What about the Barbie-doll figure? Researchers generating a computer model of a woman with Barbie-doll proportions found that her back would be too weak to support the weight of her upper body, and her body would be too narrow to contain more than half a liver and a few centimeters of bowel. A real woman built that way would suffer from chronic diarrhea and eventually die from malnutrition.

Have students take turns reading these Scripture aloud and telling the advice that is found: Psalm 45:11, Psalm 100:3, Psalm 139:13-16, Proverbs 31:30, Jeremiah 1:5.

Notes

1. http://healthymind.com/s-porn-stats.html (accessed November 2007).

2. Stephen Arterburn and Fred Stoeker, *Every Young Man's Battle* (Colorado Springs, CO: WaterBrook Press), p 109.

3. Dave Root, "Is Masturbation a Sin?" *Christian Evangelism, Healing and Teaching Resources.* http://www.layhands.com/IsMasturbationASin.htm (accessed November 2007).

Dating, Kissing, Sex & Stuff

Session 3: Is It Really Worth It?

Goal of the Session

To help kids to count the cost of having sex before marriage. All day you have been asking kids to process and wrestle with what they think and believe about sex, and now you want them to know some facts. There is a price to pay for not doing things God's way. In this session, they will discover the price and determine for themselves if it is worth paying.

Preparation for the Session

- Make a copy of the Sex Survey (pp. 196-197) for each student, and collect pens or pencils.
- Purchase the video "Sex Still Has a Price Tag" by Pam Stenzel. You must have it! It is the best video out there on the subject. It will rock your world, your kids world and the world of your adult leaders. Order this video from www.PamStenzel.com.

Sex Survey

Pass out the Sex Survey and give the kids about 10 minutes to complete it. Tell them that the correct answers will be revealed on the video they are about to view. Have the room darkened as the video plays and ask the kids to really listen and consider what is being said. Set a serious tone for this session that allows them to really soak in what Pam is saying.

Video

Have the room darkened as the video plays and ask the kids to really listen and consider what is being said. Pam talks about the physical, emotional and spiritual consequences of sex outside of marriage. Although many of your kids may have had sex education courses, they've never heard this. It is intense, however, so be prepared!

Play the video "Sex Still Has a Price Tag" by Pam Stenzel.

Discussion

After the video, go over the correct answers to the sex survey and review the high points of the video. Then break the kids into their small groups for discussion about the content that has been presented.

Sex Survey: Sex Has a Price Tag

1. The media tells us a lot about having sex. Which responses are true and which are false?

Everybody's doin' it! _____ T _____ F

It is fun! _____ T _____ F

Feels great! _____ T _____ F

No consequences! _____ T _____ F

2. What are God's boundaries for sex?

Dated at least a month

Never on the first date

Only for procreation (having kids)

Marriage

Love

3. There are consequences, or a cost, to having sex outside of marriage.

Never

Sometimes

Most of the time

Always

4. What is the biggest fear that teens have about premarital sex?

_____
_____
_____
_____

5. If you have premarital sex, the odds of contracting a disease are how many times the chance of becoming pregnant?

8 times

4 times

Equal

6. Of teenage girls who choose to parent, how many of them will live below the poverty level?

_____ out of 10.

7. Of teenage girls who choose to parent, how many of them will NOT graduate from college?

_____ out of 10.

8. What is the number one indication of poverty in American households today?

_____
_____

9. In the last eight years, what is the percentage increase in the number of couples who are unable to have children?

_____
_____

10. How many STDs does the average pregnant teen girl carry?

_____
_____

11. How much financial aid is provided every year to support teenage girls who are parents?

30 million

300 million

30 billion

300 billion

12. Girls on birth control are _____ times more likely to get an STD.

13. Abortion should be OK (circle one):

Always

Never

In cases of rape

In cases of incest

14. How many requests for adoption go unanswered each year in the United States?

100 thousand

.5 million

1.5 million

2 million

15. There are two categories, or general types of STDs. The first is bacterial. What is the second?

_____

_____

16. What is the main difference between these two types of STDs?

_____

_____

17. In ONE DAY how many teens contract a STD?

_____

18. How many teens and COLLEGE STUDENTS IN THEIR 20s contract an STD DAILY in this country?

_____

_____

19. In the 1950s we knew of how many STDs?

_____

20. Today, how many STDs do we know of?

_____

21. Of the STDs that are prevalent in teens today, what percentage of those cannot be cured?

_____

22. What is the number one STD found in America today?

_____

_____

23. In 90 percent of the cases, what are the symptoms of Chlamydia?

_____

_____

_____

_____

24. What is the most severe consequence for women (or your future wife) who contract Chlamydia?

_____

_____

25. What STD results in death for the most women each year?

_____

26. What percentage of sexually active high school and college students have genital warts?

_____

27. Of all people over the age of 12, 1 out of _____ have Herpes.

28. Herpes can be cured. _____ T   _____ F

29. One out of _____ teens has an STD.

Circle one: 2   4   8   10

30. Among teens once they decide to have sex, how long does the average relationship last?

1 week

3 weeks

6 months

1 year

2 years

31. What is the average number of sexual partners for sexually active people under 30?

_____

Dating, Kissing, Sex & Stuff

Session 3: Small Group

Goal of the Small Group

To help kids realize the serious consequences that result from sex outside of God's boundaries.

Discussion

Ask the questions below and invite student responses.

1. What is one thing you learned from Pam on the video that you didn't know before?

2. Did Pam challenge any previously held thoughts, beliefs or assumptions you had about sex?

3. What is something you are looking forward to in the future of your life? Goals or dreams?

4. Do you think the consequences of having sex could prevent you from experiencing that?

5. How would you feel if you had to tell your future husband or wife that you had an STD (Sexually Transmitted Disease)?

6. What if they told you that? How would you respond? What would you say?

7. How many of you know someone in your grade that is having sex?

8. We have heard a lot about the reasons you should wait to have sex. What are some of the reasons someone would not want to wait?

9. Do you think those reasons are worth the price? Why or why not?

198

Dating, Kissing, Sex & Stuff

Session 4: You Make the Call

Goal of the Session

To give the kids a chance to make some decisions, set some goals and establish some boundaries. It is a time when they can go before God in worship and hear directly from His Word as you share final thoughts, reflections and challenges.

Preparing for the Session

- Prepare to have a worship band play and a worship leader lead the kids in worship with music they know and like.
- Make a copy of a Commitment Card (p. 202) for each person.
- Provide stationery, envelopes, scissors and pens. Collect a Bible and two baskets or containers.
- Work hard to make the setting of this session special, intimate and worshipful. Consider using decorations from your church's wedding ministry to decorate the space as if the kids were arriving at a wedding ceremony. A dimly lit room provides intimacy and a feeling of safety for this closing session.

Worship

Begin this time with the best possible worship experience for your students. Give them a chance to really connect with and feel the presence of the Lord. Setting the tone with worship that really connects with the kids is essential. It just makes sense that when kids connect with God in a personal and intimate way their hearts are more open to where He wants to lead them.

Challenge

This is your chance to summarize the retreat with your kids, revisit the key points that you want to be fresh in their minds and then really challenge them to have their own convictions. Be honest with your students about the difficulty of staying sexually pure in our world today. Talk about the struggles they will face as they continue on through high school, college and early adult life. Explain to them that it may be nearly impossible for them to experience success in this area of their lives without the supernatural power of God.

The following are additional points from Scripture that you might want to emphasize. Read 1 Corinthians 10:13 aloud: "No temptation has seized you except what is common to man. And God is faithful; he will not let you be tempted beyond what you can bear. But when you are tempted, he will also provide a way out so that you can stand up under it."

Discuss this Scripture one section at a time:

- "No temptation has seized you except what is common to man." Although the challenges and temptations that lie ahead are huge and overwhelming to you, to God they are simply common struggles—struggles He's seen before and struggles He'll see again; struggles that don't shock Him, don't scare Him and can't defeat Him.
- "And God is faithful; he will not let you be tempted beyond what you can bear." God will walk with you as you face these struggles. He won't abandon you to be crushed or defeated. He won't leave you on your own. No, He will be there to give you the discipline, the power and the strength to be victorious.
- "But when you are tempted, he will also provide a way out so that you can stand up under it." You will have to rely on Him. You will have to stand up under Him and lean on His power. Because God doesn't say that you won't

have struggles. He doesn't guarantee that you won't be tempted. And He doesn't say you will have the strength to resist on your own. But He does guarantee that He will be your strength if you rely on Him!

Commitment Letters and Cards

Explain to the students that they now have two opportunities. The first opportunity is to write a letter to themselves about their experience on this weekend, their sexual boundaries and expectations before marriage and goals they have for themselves in this area. Encourage them to be as specific and honest as possible since no one but them will read their letters. Explain that you will mail the letters in a few months.

The second opportunity is to make a commitment to God by signing an abstinence Commitment Card. The card is divided into two halves, separated by a dotted line. On one part of the card is a place for the students to sign their name and date. Students should keep this portion for themselves as a reminder of their commitment. On the other part of the card, students are asked to fill out some personal information so that you can keep track of who has made a commitment and be a source of support and encouragement to them in the future.

Challenge the students NOT to fill out a card unless they are absolutely serious about it. Encourage real commitments from kids, not half-hearted commitment from kids who feel pressured in the moment but who ultimately have no serious intentions of following through.

As the worship band plays, students write letters, address envelopes, and sign cards.

Concluding the Event or Retreat

At some discreet location in the room set out two baskets or containers. After allowing time for students to write letters and/or complete and cut apart cards, invite students to place their letters and/or cards in the baskets or containers. Designate one basket or container for the letters, now sealed in the self-addressed envelopes, and designate the other basket or container for the information part of the Commitment Card. This closing ceremony is a high point of the event or retreat and the kids will really be impacted by their participation.

Commitment Card

Name:

Address:

Phone:

E-mail:

From today forward, I commit to abstinence from sex outside of God's boundaries until I'm married. I recognize that keeping this commitment will protect me from the painful consequences of sex outside of marriage.

Date:

Signature:

Commitment Card

Name:

Address:

Phone:

E-mail:

From today forward, I commit to abstinence from sex outside of God's boundaries until I'm married. I recognize that keeping this commitment will protect me from the painful consequences of sex outside of marriage.

Date:

Signature:

Parent Session A

What Are Kids Really Facing?

Goal of the Session

To encourage, motivate and inform your parents, and to create a sense of urgency in dealing with this topic.

For a variety of reasons, most parents do not have an open dialogue with their children about sexual struggles, temptations, values or convictions. Kids are generally left to navigate this area of life alone, which is one of the main reasons many students get into trouble. This is an "in your face" session for parents and I invite you to boldly challenge them to get over their fears, step outside their comfort zones and enter into their child's sexual struggles and decisions.

This session will be an overlap of what you also cover with the students. This will keep parents in-the-know on what you are teaching and telling their kids, as well as create a common experience. Knowing what was covered and experienced on the retreat or event will pave the way for parents to follow up and interact with their child on the subject.

Preparation for the Session

- Purchase the PowerPoint Game "Animal Sex." This game is part of *The Power of Sex: A 6-Week Super Series* by Doug Fields. Order this product online at simplyyouthministry.com.
- Make a copy of the Sex Survey (pp. 196-197) for each parent and collect pens or pencils.
- Purchase the video "Sex Still Has a Price Tag" by Pam Stenzel. You must have it! It is the best video out there on the subject. It will rock your world, your kids' world and the world of your adult leaders. Order this video from www.PamStenzel.com.
- Make a copy of the Parent Resources page (p. 208) for each parent.

Welcome and Ice Breaker

Introduce yourself and other staff.

Lead parents in the same trivia game ice breaker you used with the kids. This ice breaker is a PowerPoint Game called "Animal Sex." This game presents interesting trivia and facts about all kinds of animals having sex. The game is a little risqué, but it will loosen up your crowd and help them feel comfortable.

Explain It

Explain to the parents that the following ground rules were laid down at the start of the retreat for their students and most, if not all of them, also work for the time they will spend with you as well.

- Schmoopiness. Although the title of our weekend is DKSS, we will not actually be participating in dating, kissing, sex and stuff on the weekend. (Sorry if any of you are disappointed!) This rule means that if you are here with your spouse, you are not going to be able to kiss, cuddle or hold hands this weekend. Boys are blue, girls are pink and these colors won't mix to form PURPLE! Sorry!

- Maturity. Act like adults! Explain to your parents that this is a weekend filled with adult content. Explain that some of the material discussed may make them feel uncomfortable and how they react and respond to those feelings is what shows maturity.

Tell them that they may be tempted to make jokes, laugh, giggle, make inappropriate comments to relieve the uncomfortable tension or feelings they might have, but maturity is being able to deal with those feelings, understanding that they are natural and normal when discussing this subject matter. Challenge your parents to step up their maturity and act like adults. They will respond!

- Confidentiality. This is a closed weekend in terms of sharing. As leaders we are going to respect anything you share with us this weekend by keeping it confidential, and we expect you to show the same respect to each other. What is shared in this community stays here! (This is the one and only way in which our retreat resembles Las Vegas.) Your ability to do this is another way you show respect for one another and personal maturity.

- Authenticity. Challenge your parents to be REAL not just RIGHT. Ultimately, for the most part we all know the right answers this weekend, but that is not really what we are interested in. This is a safe environment for you to not just be right but be real. We want to hear and wrestle with what you really think, with the questions you really have, with the doubts you sometimes have and with the worries you really have about your child's behaviors or the behavior your child may just be considering. The more authentic you are this weekend, the more you will get out of it.

Inspire Them

Tell the three stories of adolescent experiences that were told in Session 1 (see pp. 181-183). Explain how each parent's child fits into one of these three groups. It is great for parents to understand the range of experiences different kids are having and also understand that no matter where their son or daughter is, this retreat is for them. In other words, just like the kids, Mom and Dad need to know why this retreat is for their child.

We believe, and statistics support, that the number one influence in the life of your kids is you! Not just in terms of life in general, but also when it comes to sexual choices. Like it or not, your communication with your child, or lack there of is having an impact.

We know that sex can be a very uncomfortable topic of discussion between parent and child. We also know that many of you had little or no interaction with your own parents about sexual pressures, temptations and decisions. So this is new territory for many of you. That is why we are here to encourage, empower and support you as you enter into the very scary world of teenage sex and sexuality. We want you to know you are not alone. We want you to know that your kids need you to be brave. We want you to know that even

when it doesn't feel like it, you are making an impact.

We believe that what you say, and what you don't say has a profound impact on your kids. What I mean by that is:

- Avoidance doesn't make things go away;
- Proclaiming, "Don't have sex until you're married, don't have sex until you're married, don't have sex until you're married" is not what they need;
- If you can really share your thoughts, experiences and, most importantly, values with your kids it will make a difference.

One of the biggest fears that adults have is when it comes to open dialogue with their child about sex. Our message at this church is unapologetically that:

- God created sex;
- Sex is good;
- Sex is a gift from God for our enjoyment;
- Sex is intended to be experienced within the marriage relationship only.

So the question that comes up from parents more than any other question is, "What if that's not my experience? What if my wife and I didn't wait until we were married? What if I haven't had sex with just one person? What do I do then? What do I tell my kids when they ask me?" Your thought here might be "If I don't have the discussion, I won't have to answer the question, so I'll just avoid it."

These are very fair, real and honest feelings. It is hard to face our failures, especially with our kids. But let me challenge you with two things:

Is this about you or your child? Is your discomfort worth the peril of your child navigating the dangers of today's sexual path alone, without help, support or guidance from you?

How you answer the question is up to you, but have an answer ready because they will ask. Talk about it as a couple, come to agreement and move forward in talking to your kids. My suggestion is to be discreetly honest. You don't have to share all the gory details, but tell the truth. Authenticity goes a long way with kids and if you are willing to be vulnerable and transparent with them, they may just open up with you when they are struggling.

Survey and Video

Pass out the Sex Survey and give the parents about 10 minutes to complete it. Tell them that their children will be taking the same survey and their scores will be compared. Also explain to them that the correct answers will be revealed to them on the video they are about to view.

After parents complete the survey, play the video "Sex Still has a Price Tag" by Pam Stenzel. Pam talks about the physical, emotional and spiritual consequences of sex outside of marriage. It is intense so tell your parents to be prepared.

A Letter to Your Child

Now that your parents are scared to death about what their kids are facing in our world today, they are really ready to listen. Remind them that although Pam is great, hearing her one time at an eighth grade retreat will only go so far in the lives of kids facing enormous temptation now and in the future. However, if alongside experiences like this one is a steady stream of parental involvement, care, concern and family values rooted in Christ, your kids might just have a chance at experiencing sex and relationships the best way, God's way.

So where can you start? More than just information, your kids need you to share your heart with them. They need to know how much you care before they care how much you know. They need to hear how much you love them and why you want them to make the choices you want them to make, even if they are different choices than you made. This kind of communication doesn't happen by handing them a book or sitting them down in front of a video.

Give your parents a homework assignment: write a letter to your child. It should be a letter full of affirmation, love and acceptance. Parents can write about the hopes and dreams they have for their child. Parents can share what they want for their child in terms of sexual choices and why. Parents can express their willingness and availability to help them any time they need help or just someone to talk with.

Have the parents write the letter at home, seal it in an envelope addressed to their child and turn it in the next morning. In several months, mail those letters!

Take It Home

Distribute the Parent Resources page to help parents who want to do or read more about helping their child through the teen years.

Suggested Resources

Dobson, Dr. James. *Preparing for Adolescence* (book, family workbook, group guide, CDs). Ventura, CA: Gospel Light, 2006.

Garth, Lakita. *The Naked Truth About Sex, Love and Relationships* (book, DVD, leader's guide, student's guide). Ventura, CA: Regal Books, 2007.

Find additional resources at www.faithbeginsathome.com.

Video
- *Sex Still Has a Price Tag*. Order from www.PamStenzel.com.

Medical Concerns
- www.medinstitute.org—The Medical Institute for Sexual Health is an organization that has a tremendous heart for the health and well-being of all. It is committed to teaching people how to make good choices and adopt healthy behaviors that enable them to achieve their highest potential.
- www.cdc.gov—The Centers for Disease Control and Prevention (CDC) is one of the 13 major operating components of the Department of Health and Human Services (HHS), which is the principal agency in the United States government for protecting the health and safety of all Americans
- www.standupgirl.com—A site for teenage girls who find themselves pregnant and alone.
- www.pregnancycenters.org—A site that will give you solid guidance and send you to other places where you can get caring help.
- www.pathwayofhope.org—Pathway of Hope's Youth and Family Services is a state-licensed, residential treatment facility for girls, ages ten through eighteen. They are a non-denominational, non-profit, Christian organization, combining professional excellence with Christian values and providing twenty-four hour care and professional treatment in a relaxed home setting.

Pornography Help
- www.XXXChurch.com—A site that addresses the issues, provides help and accountability for teens and adults faced with the temptation of pornography.

Books
- Arterburn, Stephen and Fred Stoeker. *Every Young Man's Battle*. Colorado Springs, CO: WaterBrook Press, 2002.
- Dobson, James. *Preparing for Adolescence*. Ventura, CA: Gospel Light, 2006.
- Ethridge, Shannon and Stephen Arterburn. *Every Young Woman's Battle*. Colorado Springs, CO: WaterBrook Press, 2004.
- Garth, Lakita. *The Naked Truth About Sex, Love and Relationships*. Ventura, CA: Regal Books, 2007.
- Lochner, Todd. *How Far Is Too Far*. City, STATE: Brown Books, 2004.
- Smalley, Michael, Amy Smalley and Mike Yorkey. *Don't Date Naked*. Carol Stream, IL: Tyndale House, 2003.

Teen Communication
- www.cpyu.org—The Center for Parent/Youth Understanding provides many resources and ideas that help parents understand, talk and listen to their kids. Read about youth culture and look for the section titled Parent Resources.

Promise Rings
- www.lifeway.com/tlw/—True Love Waits is a link for promise rings, resources and more.

Parent Session B
(For Parents and Students)

Let's Talk About Sex

Goal of Session

To break the ice and to get parents and kids talking.

Preparing for the Session

- Shoot a video of staff and volunteers from your church simply saying only the word "sex." Get old people and young people, men and women. Get as many people as you can and it will be hilarious! Get the least likely people expected and get them to do it "for the kids." If you can, have the senior pastor and his wife say the last "sex" together and then kiss for a closing.
- Snacks for students.

Parent Question and Discussion

As the parents gather before the students join the group, ask if they have any questions. Be ready to answer questions related to the event. For questions related to the topic of the event, try to become more of a facilitator allowing parents to answer questions for each other on the topic and share ideas. Share your thoughts and then say things like, "Does anyone else have any ideas on that?" This sharing will probably happen naturally.

Students Arrive

When the students arrive, have a separate room for them to gather in before you bring them in to be with their folks. Provide snacks for them to munch on while they wait (it makes them happy!). When it is time bring them all in, ask them to sit with their family.

Explain It

Explain that it may be a bit uncomfortable during the session. Talk about how it was uncomfortable when the students first gathered, but when everyone settled in it got easier. In the same way, it was a bit uncomfortable for the parents when they first gathered, but they too got used to the subject matter. But now that parents and kids are together, it may be really awkward sitting next to each other while talking about the subject of sex. Reassure them that it is OK and good to talk about sex like this in the church setting.

Show the video you prepared and watch tension fly out of the room as the laughter begins.

Then explain that, although it can be hard, parents and kids should have open honest communication about sex. Tell the students that you can guarantee that their parents know more about sex than they and their friends do. Tell them that your goal is to get them started on a conversation that you hope will continue when you get home. Assure them that these questions will be easy and hopefully won't be too embarrassing as they test the waters.

Practice It

Ask families to talk together as you lead them with some discussion questions. Give families a few minutes to share as you ask the following questions:

- Ask each family member to share with each other, on a scale of 1 to 10 (1 being low and 10 being high), How uncomfortable are you discussing the subject of sex with your parents/son or daughter? Why?
- Ask each family member to share some things from their Sex Survey results (one question you got right, one you got wrong) or something you were surprised to learn from the video.
- Parents, share how, when and where you first learned about sex and what your reaction was.
- Parents, share who first told you about sex. What happened?
- Ask each family member to share what they think each of the following believe and say about sex: the media? God? You?
- Parents, share with your son/daughter a hope and a worry you have concerning their future relationships and sexual experiences.

Take It Home

Encourage parents and kids to keep the discussion going at home.

Looking into the Future
(Spiritual Gifts)

Target Age of Children

Teenagers

Goal of Take It Home Event

To examine and explore spiritual gifts God has given children and the possibilities God may have in using these gifts in the future.

Preparing for the Event

- As a part of this event, you will need to interview either a pastor and his or her secretary or a business professional and his or her secretary.
- Make copies of Me and My Spiritual Gifts (pp. 215-216). You will need to make one copy per person, plus one additional copy per family.

Explain It

Begin by having everyone stand in the center of the room. Explain that you are going to call out the names of two options and that everyone will need to choose which option they like or agree with the most. Say, "After hearing both options, if you agree with the first option stand on the left side of the room. If you like or agree with the second option, stand on the right side of the room."

Call out the following options (be creative and add your own ideas if you wish) and have people move to the appropriate side of the room:

- Which do you like better—vanilla ice cream or chocolate ice cream?
- Which do you like better—pepperoni pizza or sausage pizza?
- Which do you like better—healthy salad or a double cheeseburger with bacon?
- Are you a morning person or a night owl?
- Would you rather work with your hands or with people?
- When a stoplight turns yellow, do you speed up and power through or hit your brakes and stop?
- Which would you rather watch on TV—a reality show or sports?

At the conclusion of the activity, have everyone be seated. Share a story of when you first recognized a gift your child or a young child had. You may choose to tell the story from Mark Holmen.

> I knew my daughter had the gift of administration when she was less than one year old. If we put a newspaper next to her, she would sort it page by page and put the entire paper on her left. Then she would sort it again and move it page by page to the right. She was clearly an organizer from the very beginning. This activity kept her busy for hours!

Then have the families take turns completing the following sentence starters:

- A gift or ability I have had since an early age is . . .
- When I was a child I wanted to be a . . .
- My favorite subject in school was or is . . .
- My most enjoyable or comfortable thing to do is . . .

Lead the group in a discussion of Scripture verses related to spiritual gifts. Read 1 Corinthians 12:1 aloud. God wants us to know and understand what spiritual gifts are. Ask, "How many of you have ever gone through a gift inventory?" (DiSC Personality Profile, Myers Briggs, etc.) "Has anyone done a spiritual gift inventory?"

Let's find out what the Bible says spiritual gifts are. Read 1 Corinthians 12:4-11 aloud. Ask, "What are some of the gifts listed in this passage? Is this an exclusive list?" (No.) "What is the key concept?" (There are different kinds of gifts, but all these are the work of the same Spirit and He gives them to each of us just as He determines.)

Read 1 Corinthians 12:12-26 and ask, "What is the key to how we value the different spiritual gifts we have?" Equality is the governing principle. But does our society value gifts equally? Do we value schoolteachers as much as athletes? Do we value professional care-givers who work with the elderly in nursing homes as much as music or movie stars? Ask volunteers to answer, "What do you think is the reason for the difference?"

To focus on God's purpose for spiritual gifts, read 1 Corinthians 12:27-31 aloud. Ask, "What is God's plan for giving us different gifts? Could the church survive if it only had teachers and no workers?" Discuss ways your church uses the different gifts people have.

Inspire Them

Introduce the guests you invited (a pastor and his or her secretary or a business professional and his or her secretary). After introducing them, ask a series of questions such as the following:

- Would each of you share with us when you first sensed the call to be a pastor or secretary?
- When and how did God call you to serve in our congregation?
- Pastor, what spiritual gifts does

your secretary have? How do those spiritual gifts compliment and help you serve as our pastor?

- Secretary, what spiritual gifts does our pastor have? How do those spiritual gifts compliment and help you serve as his or her secretary?

Close the interview with a time of prayer, praising God for bringing these two people, with different gifts, to serve and lead your church.

Model It

Hand out the Me and My Spiritual Gifts worksheet. Begin by having each person write his or her name, and the names of their family members at the top of the page. Give them five minutes to individually go through the list of spiritual gifts and check the spiritual gifts they think they and their family members have.

When everyone has finished, give each family one more blank Me and My Spiritual Gifts page. Ask each person to tally their results for each member of the family.

Practice It

Have the family go through the following questions based on the spiritual gifts inventory they just took:

- Is there unanimous agreement on some of the spiritual gifts?

- Is there disagreement on certain gifts?
- What spiritual gifts do you have in common with one another?
- How can you use these spiritual gifts in the career you have or are considering?
- How can we or are we using these spiritual gifts within our church?

End the activity with a time of prayer praising God for the different ways He has gifted us all.

Take It Home

Remind your families spiritual gifts may change from year to year. Encourage them to do this activity again in a year or two to see how things have changed or stayed the same. Keep your results and it will provide a fun comparison.

Suggested Resources

Kise, Jane and Kevin Johnson. *Find Your Fit*. Minneapolis, MN: Bethany House, 1999.

Wagner, C. Peter. *Discover Your Spiritual Gifts*. Ventura, CA: Regal Books, 2005.

Wagner, C. Peter. *Your Spiritual Gifts*. Ventura, CA: Regal Books, 2005.

Find additional resources at www.faithbeginsathome.com.

Me and My Spiritual Gifts

GIFTS OF ACTION	YOU	NAME	NAME	NAME
Administration—This person is able to understand and set goals for various groups. This person is able to plan, organize and get things done.	___	___	___	___
Craftsmanship—This person can use his/her hands to build things.	___	___	___	___
Arts and Crafts—This person can use his/her hands in creative and artistic ways.	___	___	___	___
Encouragement—This person has the ability to give words of comfort, support to people in a way that helps them.	___	___	___	___
Leadership—This person has the ability to motivate and direct people to get things done.	___	___	___	___
Music-Vocal—The ability to sing joyfully. The next American Idol!	___	___	___	___
Music-Instrumental—The ability to joyfully play an instrument.	___	___	___	___

GIFTS OF THE HEART

	YOU	NAME	NAME	NAME
Faith—The ability to have confidence in God in all circumstances.	___	___	___	___
Giving—The enjoyment of sharing your resources to help others.	___	___	___	___
Hospitality—The joy of welcoming people into your home and serving them.	___	___	___	___
Mercy—The ability to care for those who are hurting or in need.	___	___	___	___
Serving—The ability to identify and meet needs in the community or world.	___	___	___	___

GIFTS OF INSPIRATION

	YOU	NAME	NAME	NAME
Prayer—The enjoyment of praying frequently and specifically for others.	___	___	___	___

	YOU	NAME	NAME	NAME
Teaching—The ability to explain things to others in a way they can understand.	____	____	____	____
Wisdom—The ability to offer sound advice.	____	____	____	____
Writing—The ability to put your thoughts and ideas into meaningful words that influence others.	____	____	____	____

GIFTS OF PROCLAMATION

Discernment—The ability to know right from wrong, good and evil, truth and error.	____	____	____	____
Evangelism—The ability and passion to easily tell others about Jesus.	____	____	____	____
Knowledge—The ability to discover new truths, ideas and information.	____	____	____	____

Section 4

Faith Begins at Home Sermon Series

The following are sermon outlines with PowerPoint slides for a five-part sermon series entitled Faith Begins at Home— The Home Makeover with Christ at the Center. The sermon series was written to complement Pastor Mark Holmen's book, *Faith Begins at Home*, which provides small group discussion questions at the end of each chapter to keep your small groups engaged in the series during the week. This sermon series is also a great opportunity to launch some intergenerational family small groups in your church.

- Consider dividing your church into small groups of 8 to 10 people for five weeks with each small group having youth, parents and grandparents meeting together during the week to discuss how to bring Christ into the center of their home.
- Another idea is to spread the five-part sermon series out over five months and designate one Sunday each month to focus on Faith Begins at Home. This provides more time for your small groups to meet and implement some of the practical ideas suggested in each chapter.
- And finally, this sermon series can serve to setup and launch a mentoring program as described in Take It Home Event: Mentoring—Establishing Another Voice.

This sermon series has been provided in outline form allowing you the opportunity to customize it to your situation adding your own thoughts, ideas and personal illustrations. The PowerPoint slides can also be customized to match the changes and additions you make.

Faith Begins at Home
Sermon Outline #1: The Home Makeover
(Text: Joshua 24)

I. Opening

A. Discuss how adept we have become at building and rebuilding homes.

    1. Discuss the Extreme Home Makeover television show and how, in one week, they completely rebuild a home that was one of the worst in town to one of the best in town.

    2. In this five-part series we are going to discussing another makeover that needs to happen and that's rebuilding your home with Christ at the center!

        a. Make sure your congregation understands that this series is for everyone, not just families with children. A single person, senior citizen, etc, needs Christ at the center of the home they live in.

        b. Discuss that one USA Today article described that we have over 28 forms of family today. This series is for every form of family no matter what shape, size, age or demographic!

II. Examining Our Condition

A. The first thing the Extreme Makeover television show does is to go through the home, in its current condition, that they will be making over. As they go through it, you vividly see how necessary a makeover is needed.

B. Why is this five-part series needed? While we have become very adept at building homes, we have become worse at building families with Christ at the center.

C. Let's take a look at the condition of families today. Share the following results of the Search Institute Effective Christian Education survey. (Used by permission of Search Institute, 615 First Avenue NE, Minneapolis, MN 55413; www.search-institute.org.)

    1. Percentage of churched youth who view their mom as very religious? (48%)

2. Percentage of churched youth who view their dad as very religious? (23%)

3. Percentage of churched youth who have experienced either family devotions, prayer or Bible reading in the home? (27%)

4. Percentage of churched youth who have experienced a family service project? (29%)

D. And remember these are the results of churched youth! Imagine what the results would be for unchurched youth?

E. Do we need an extreme home makeover with Christ at the center today?

F. Today our extreme makeover begins with The Home Makeover.

1. Part 2 will be The Parent Makeover

2. Part 3 will be The Child Makeover

3. Part 4 will be The Extended Family Makeover

4. Part 5 will be The Church Makeover

G. Let's get started with our makeover or as Ty Pennington would say, "Let's Do It!"

III. Joshua 24 Background

A. Provide some background that sets up chapter 24 of Joshua.

1. Joshua is older in age, like a grandparent (23:1).

2. God has fulfilled his promise to bring the Israelites into a great land and delivered them from their enemies.

3. Life is good for the people; they have food, clothing, housing, freedom and prosperity.

4. Question for us to consider: Do we have life pretty good today?

5. Yet we are still in need of a makeover. And that's exactly what Joshua was trying to help his people avoid.

6. And in his final, "deathbed" message Joshua gives us some precious things to consider that will serve as the key to a successful home makeover.

IV. Home Makeover Key #1—Remember

A. Read Joshua 24:1-13 (only verses 1-5 are on the PowerPoint slides).

1. You may not need to read all 13 verses to get your point across.

2. Emphasize each time the text reads, "I took, I gave, I assigned, I sent, I afflicted, I brought, I gave, I destroyed, I delivered, etc."

3. Why did Joshua spend so much time retelling the story?

4. Point: When you have life pretty good, it's easy to forget God.

5. Have we forgotten God and everything He has done for us?

6. Talk about how the culture you live in keeps people so busy that they no longer have time for God. Provide examples of how your culture has squeezed God and things like prayer, worship, etc. out of how you live.

7. The results: We no longer REMEMBER God or what God has done for us. We have lost our personal connection with God.

   a. Have the people watch a "Who is God?" or "Who is Jesus" street interview video clip which depicts how much confusion exists regarding who God is today.

   b. Sermonspice.com has good video clips you can purchase.

8. The reality—Families are hurting and needing a makeover.

   a. Unfortunately they are turning everywhere else for help, to Oprah, Dr. Phil, psychics, (list others in your community), etc.

   b. Yet they aren't turning to God because they've forgotten what God has done for them and what God can do for them!

   c. Remember—This is the God who created the heavens and the earth, who parted the Red Sea, who made the blind man see and raised Lazarus from the dead. If He can do all that, He can probably help you and your family!

   d. Practical Application Question—Has your family forgotten God?

IV. Home Makeover Key #2—Choose

A. Read Joshua 24:13-18.

B. You and your family have a choice to make.

   1. Option #1—Serve the gods of this world—materialism, money, fast paced life, busyness, etc.

      a. These gods put you on a treadmill going through life.

    b. Where do treadmills get you?

  2. Option #2—Serve the one true God.

    a. This God loves you, created you, knows you better than you know yourself, has plans to prosper you and not to harm you, and intends for you and your family to enjoy long life.

    b. And His ways lead to everlasting life for you and your family!

C. The Choice Begins with You

  1. The passage reads, "AS FOR ME . . ." before it says anything about the household.

  2. The point: You can't pass something on to your children you don't have yourself.

  3. Provide a personal story of a habit, statement, or tradition you have passed on to your children and/or something that was passed on to you from your parents. For example, my parents taught me to put salt on my pepperoni pizza and now my daughter does the same thing. It doesn't get any better than this!

  4. In the same way, if we want our children to have a faith that impacts the decisions they make and the life they choose, we need to have a faith that impacts our decisions and the life we live.

  5. Go through the Significant Religious Influences survey (Early Childhood Education study, Search Institute, Minneapolis, MN.)

Mother	81% male	74% female
Father	61% male	50% female
Pastor	57% male	44% female
Grandparent	30% male	29% female
Sunday school	26% male	26% female
Youth group	24% male	25% female
Church camp	20% male	28% female
Retreats	11% male	17% female

  6. As you can see, mother and father are 2-3 times more influential than any church program.

  7. Share one or more of the following quotes;

    a. "For all their specialized training, church professionals realize that if a child is not receiving basic Christian nurture in the home, even the best teachers and curriculum will have minimal impact. Once-a-week exposure simply cannot compete with daily experience where personal formation is concerned." (Marjorie Thompson, *Family, The Forming Center*, rev. ed. Nashville, TN: Upper Room Books, 1996, back cover.)

b. "Most teenagers and their parents may not realize it, but a lot of research in the sociology of religion suggest that the most important social influence in shaping young people's religious lives is the religious life modeled and taught to them by their parents." (Christian Smith, *Soul Searching*, New York, NY: Oxford University Press, 2005, p. 56.)

c. And finally my favorite quote from Dr. Roland Martinson of Luther Seminary: "What we ought to do is let the kids drop their parents off at church, train the parents and send them back into their mission field, their home, to grow Christians!"

8. Practical Application Question—Have you and your family made the "As for me and my household we will serve the Lord" choice?

a. The good news is that it's never too late! Expand on this point talking about how our God is a God of second chances.

b. The choice you make today can impact your family for generations to come. Share a personal story of how a decision your grandparents or great-grandparents made is still impacting your family today.

VI. Home Makeover Key #3—Remain

A. Read Joshua 24:25-27.

B. We will need help remaining "As for me and my household we will serve the Lord" families. Talk about how Satan is not going to leave you or your family alone just because you have decided to follow Jesus.

C. Joshua said, "This stone will be a witness against us"

1. What will be the witness against us in our homes?

2. Talk about establishing a home altar, hanging a cross in a prominent location or even placing a large rock somewhere in your home that will bear witness that you are a Christ-centered family.

D. That's the role of the church—to help you remain.

    1. George Barna quote "The local church should be an intimate and valuable partner in the effort to raise the coming generation of Christ's followers and church leaders, but it is the parents whom God will hold primarily accountable for the spiritual maturation of their children." (George Barna, *Transforming Children into Spiritual Champions,* Ventura, CA: Regal Books, 2003, pp. 83-84.)

    2. The role of the church is to be a lifelong partner not replacement.

    3. Share your church's passion and commitment to partner with the people of your congregation to reestablish the home as the primary place where faith is nurtured.

        a. Share any new things you will be implementing, like Take It Home events, mentoring, family small groups, etc. to strengthen your commitment to this partnership.

        b. You may also want to make the book, *Faith Begins at Home* available for purchase as a resource that will inspire, motivate and equip people to bring Christ into the center of their home.

    4. Close this portion of the message by using the "Light shining bright from our church vs. light on in every home" vision/analogy. "The role of the church is not to make sure that as you look down on this community you can see the light shining bright from our campus/facility. The role of the church is to make sure the light is shining in each and every home so the community can be lit for the world to see!"

VII. Closing Invitation

A. Whether it's your church's tradition or not, challenge/invite people to make a "As for me, and my household we will serve the Lord" commitment/decision.

B. Invite them to come forward and take/receive a rock that will serve as a symbolic reminder of the decision/commitment they made.

C. Instruct the people to take the rock home and place it in a place of prominence in their home, thereby serving as a witness against the decision/commitment they have made.

D. Close in prayer.

Faith Begins at Home
Sermon Outline #2: The Family Makeover
(Text: Deuteronomy 6)

I. Opening—Background on Deuteronomy

A. The word Deuteronomy means "repetition of the law."

B. Throughout Deuteronomy Moses is continually repeating the will and commands of God to an Israelite nation that is . . .

    1. Stubborn

    2. Me-focused

    3. Rebellious

    4. Forgetful

    5. Back and forth in obedience

    6. Sound familiar?

C. Are you or your family stubborn, me-focused, rebellious, forgetful or back and forth in obedience to God?

D. Most families today want to be healthy and strong yet the majority has gone away from having Christ and Christ-like living in the home therefore a family makeover, with Christ at the center, is needed.

E. Last week we learned that the makeover begins with a choice to be a "as for me and my household we will serve the Lord" family.

F. Now it's time for a "repetition of the law"!

II. Read Deuteronomy 6:1-2

A. Family Makeover Key #1—Long Term Vision

B. Emphasize the two "so that's". Why is Moses continually repeating the will and commands of God to the Israelites, and us today?

C. "So that" #1—"So that you, your children and your children after them"

    1. The decision you make to be an "as for me and my household we will serve the Lord" family and to live according to the will and commands of God will impact multiple generations.

    2. What do you want your children and grandchildren's families to look like?

3. Share a story of a decision your parents or grandparents made that is still impacting your family today.

D. "So that" #2—"So that you may enjoy long life"

   1. Isn't "enjoying long life" what we want most for ourselves, our children and our grandchildren?

   2. God wants this for you and your family as well!

   3. Yet, Satan is strategically attacking families because he doesn't want them to enjoy long life.

      a. Satan knows if he can get Christ, and Christ-like living out of the home, he can keep families from enjoying long life for generations to come.

      b. Satan may have done this to you and your family, but it doesn't need to stay that way anymore.

III. Read Deuteronomy 6:3-6

A. Family Makeover Key #2—You and Your . . .

B. Point out that there are two "Hear, O Israel . . ." statements.

C. "Hear, O Israel" #1—"Hear, O Israel and be careful to obey so that it may go well with you"

   1. Change "O Israel" to the name of your church. For example I would say, "Hear O people of Ventura Missionary Church!"

   2. If you want things to "go well" for you and your family you need to be careful to obey the following commands of God.

   3. If you're not careful to obey, guess what will probably happen?

   4. Use an analogy or personal story to emphasize this point. Example— "Being careful to eat healthy and exercise leads to enjoying better health in the long run."

D. "Hear, O Israel" #2—"The Lord our God, the Lord is one. Love the Lord *your* God with all *your* heart and with all *your* soul and with all *your* strength. These commandments that I give you today are to be upon *your* hearts."

   1. What one word is repeated five times in these two verses? Your.

   2. The family makeover begins with you and your commitment to carefully obey the will and commands of God.

   3. Practical Application Question—What would your family and friends

say you love with all your heart, soul and strength?

4. Remember, your children will learn to love what you love.

IV. Read Deuteronomy 6:7-9

A. Family Makeover Key #3—Talk and Walk It!

B. How do you pass faith on to our children and children's children?

C. Firs, YOU have to love the Lord with all your heart, soul and strength. You can't pass something on you don't have yourself.

D. Second, you need to talk the talk and walk the walk all the time not just at church.

E. Unfortunately this isn't happening today.

1. Go through the following statistics from the Search Institute Effective Christian Education survey. (First two are a review from last week.)

   a. Percentage of churched youth who view their mom as very religious? (48%)

   b. Percentage of churched youth who view their dad as very religious? (23%)

   c. Percentage of churched youth who have talked with mom about faith? (28%)

   d. Percentage of churched youth who have talked with dad about faith? (13%)

2. Discuss what these statistics reveal regarding how much we are talking the talk and walking the walk as Christians in our homes.

F. Why isn't faith walk and talk happening in the home?

1. Reason #1—Parents have abdicated this responsibility to the church. In the same manner that we ask people to teach our children to play soccer, piano and basketball, we expect the church to teach our children faith.

2. Reason #2—The church has enabled this abdication through programs that are church focused rather than home focused.

G. Nowhere in the Bible does it say that the way to pass on faith to our children is to drop them off at church and expect the church to teach them the faith.

H. God's Word is clear in Deuteronomy, it is the parents and grandparents who are the ones primarily responsible for passing on faith to their children and children's children.

I. Read one or more of the following quotes.

1. "Most certainly father and mother are apostles, bishops, and priests to their children, for it is they who make then acquainted with the gospel." (Martin Luther, "The Estate of Marriage, 1522" quoted in Walther Brand, ed., *Luther's Works*, Philadelphia, PA: Fortress Press, 1962, p. 46.)

2. "When a church—intentionally or not—assumes a family's responsibilities in the arena of spiritually nurturing children, it fosters an unhealthy dependence upon the church to relieve the family of its biblical responsibility." (George Barna, *Transforming Children into Spiritual Champions*, Ventura, CA: Regal Books, 2003, p. 81.)

V. Read Deuteronomy 6:13-14

A. Family Makeover Key #4—Serve Him

B. What are the gods of the world we live in? (List a few of the worldly gods, i.e. sports, money, etc.)

C. What do you fear the most as a parent or grandparent? (The unexpected death of your child or grandchild.)

D. Is there anything the gods of this world can do to help a parent who has lost a child?

1. Yet how much time do we spend as a family serving the gods of this world versus serving God?

2. Why do we spend so much time serving those gods as a family?

VI. Closing Story or Interview/Testimony

A. Close by sharing a personal experience you have had being with a grieving couple who still had hope and peace in spite of losing a child tragically. OR

B. Interview a Christian couple from your congregation who have lost a child and have them share the comfort and hope they have as a result of the decision they previously made to be an "as for me and my household we will serve the Lord" family.

C. Closing Point—That's why we serve Him!

Faith Begins at Home
Sermon Outline #3: The Child Makeover
(Text: Psalm 127)

I. Introduction

   A. What places come to your mind when you hear the phrase—"This is where it all happens"?

      1. Maybe you think of the White House in Washington, D.C. or the Oval Office.

      2. Maybe it was a sports arena where athletic games are played.

      3. If you've recently had a baby, you might picture a hospital delivery room.

      4. When we think about the spiritual life, the faith, the relationship with God that every child has and we think about "where it all happens," the primary place kids get a spiritual makeover, we must think first and foremost about our homes, about our families.

   B. Chuck Swindoll says, "The family is the place where principles are hammered and honed on the anvil of everyday living" (http://thinkexist.com [accessed November 2007]). In other words, it is the place where character is taught and caught. It is where we learn that we are loved and cared for. It is where we learn that we have worth and have something to contribute. It should be where we learn that we can be forgiven when we have failed. It is where family members show one another what God is like and how He relates to us. It is where children learn obedience so that they will understand what it means to obey God. Home is where we learn who God is and learn to love him. Home is where we learn who we are and who others are. It's where we learn to live unselfishly with other people, taking them into consideration. All of this and much more, happens primarily within the family.

   C. As we continue our series, the message this morning is entitled: "The Child Makeover" our question is: How can our children get a Christ-centered makeover?

   D. Psalm 127

   > [1] Unless the LORD builds the house,
   >   its builders labor in vain.
   >
   > Unless the LORD watches over the city,

the watchmen stand guard in vain.

[2] *In vain you rise early*
and stay up late,
toiling for food to eat—
for he grants sleep to those he loves.

[3] *Children are a heritage from the LORD,*
children a reward from him.

[4] *Like arrows in the hands of a warrior*
are children born in one's youth.

[5] *Blessed is the man*
whose quiver is full of them.
They will not be put to shame
when they contend with their enemies in the gate.

II. How can our children get a Christ-centered makeover?

A. Our children get a Christ-centered makeover when God is the foundation of our families.

1. Verse 1—Unless the LORD builds the house, its builders labor in vain.

2. "House" = Home = Family

3. And the whole point here is that God cannot make over your kids when He is a part of their life here at church.

   a. He must infiltrate your home!

   b. God wants to be the foundation of your family.

   c. He wants to be the builder, the designer.

4. In our society we are really good at outsourcing our kids.

   a. If we want our kids to play piano, we take them to piano lessons (We take them there, drop 'em off, pick them up and over time, they play piano!).

   b. If we want our kids to play soccer, we take them to soccer team.

   c. The same occurs with karate or dance.

5. The problem is, many people treat Christianity the same way.

   a. "I mean my kids hang out with (name of your children's pastor) a couple times a week."

    b. "My kids are in Sunday School every week."

    c. "I mean they are bound to get this whole God thing down."

6. Friends let me speak for (name of children's pastor, name of youth pastor), let me speak for every church and pastor alive: We can't do it for you!

7. As a family you must talk about and live out what is being taught on Sunday morning.

    a. Christ must be built into the very framework and structure of your family.

    b. Your kids, your family members must see God

        i. Determining how you spend your time and money

        ii. Changing the way you treat your neighbors

        iii. Driving you to serve those less fortunate

8. If you were to tell me that a child could either:

    a. Grow up in a family where God was a part of the home integrated into everyday family life while growing up in a church that had nothing to offer kids and families OR grow up in a family that was a part of a thriving vibrant church with amazing ministry for youth but at home God is just not present.

    b. If you make me choose, I'd go with the strong family every time!

    c. Unless the Lord builds the house, its builders labor in vain.

    d. "The family is the place where principles, where faith, where walking with Christ in the real world is hammered and honed on the anvil of everyday living." Chuck Swindoll (http://thinkexist.com [accessed November 2007].)

    e. It's where God becomes real, where he becomes more than just a subject or a skill or a class.

    f. It's where He becomes the Lord of our lives.

9. The child makeover must happen in your home!

III. Our children get a Christ-centered makeover when we understand GOD provides and protects.

    A. Verses 1b-2

> [1b] Unless the LORD watches over the city,
>   the watchmen stand guard in vain.
>
> [2] In vain you rise early
>   and stay up late,
>   toiling for food to eat—
>   for he grants sleep to those he loves.

B. Jesus said it this way: "Therefore I tell you, do not worry about your life, what you will eat or drink; or about your body, what you will wear. Is not life more important than food, and the body more important than clothes? Look at the birds of the air: they do not sow or reap or store away in barns, and yet your heavenly Father feeds them. Are you not much more valuable than they? Who of you by worrying can add a single hour to his life?" (Matthew 6:25-27)

C. Friends, believe me, this is a tough one to live out. Tell a story about a time when you felt the pressure to provide or protect your children but you knew you couldn't but God could.

D. When you have a relationship with God one of the benefits is that you don't have to carry all that weight. Jesus says, "Give it to Me."

E. "Come to me all you who are weary and burdened and I will give you rest." Matthew 11:28

F. Are you trying to drive the ship of your child's life, or have you truly relinquished the wheel? Or, let me ask it this way. In what area of your child's life do you need to give control?

G. Story—Tell a personal story of someone giving up control in their child's life and God doing a mighty work once He had control.

IV. Our children get a Christ-centered makeover when we realize they are a blessing to us and a legacy from us.

A. Those of us who have been blessed with kids have been given one of the greatest gifts of this world, but with that comes big-time responsibility. This not only applies to parents, but to all of us anytime we have the opportunity to work with, shape, mold and influence kids.

B. Story—Share a personal moment when you realized either how blessed you were to be a parent or how much responsibility you'd been given.

C. Verse 3 says—[3]Children are a heritage from the LORD.

   1. The word "heritage" here means "inheritance"—something of lasting value that is passed down from generation to generation.

2. The idea is that children are a blessing passed from God to us but that they are also what we leave behind and pass on to the next generation.

D. In the same way an archer through his arrows can influence and be a part of a battle from a distance, we can influence our world long after we are gone through the legacy of our children.

E. Again, not just talking to parents here. Obviously parents have an active role.

1. As a church, we have got to pass our faith on to the next generation and the parents of this congregation need your help.

2. Some of you have so much to offer our kids but you have convinced yourself that your time has passed or not yet come, but you also have been given a role leaving a legacy through the children and youth of (your church's name).

F. Story—Share about an older or single adult in your congregation making a difference with young people.

V. Our children get a Christ-centered makeover when families stand strong in the face of life's challenges.

A. Last half of verse 5 says:

> 5 They will not be put to shame
>   when they contend with their enemies in the gate.

B. The city gate was the place:

1. Where business was conducted,

2. Where judgments were made (a courthouse of sorts),

3. Where people often met their adversaries.

C. Do you think the family has a few adversaries today?

1. Parents' long working hours

2. Separation of extended family

3. Divorce, drugs, sex, alcohol

4. Television and video games

D. Kids see real character when problems arise

1. Anyone can be a good role model when things are going smooth.

    2. How does your family do when facing a challenge?

        a. When you get lost on vacation

        b. When a pipe breaks and your upstairs bathroom floods

        c. When schedules conflict

        d. When you're running late for church

E. Tell a story of a time when you lost it (people connect with pastors who blow it). Or tell a story of a time one of your parents lost it.

F. House on the Rock (Matthew 7)

    1. There are two kinds of houses (families)

        a. Families built on rock

        b. Families built on sand

        c. Families built on God

        d. Families that aren't

    2. These two houses may not look that different much, if not most, of the time.

        a. You look at two families

            i. Hard-working

            ii. Strong values

            iii. Honest

        b. But you will notice the difference when the storms of life show up and things get rough. That's when the foundation of building your house on the rock of Jesus Christ will really make a noticeable difference.

G. Tell a story of a family going through a hard time and leaning on the strength of Christ to get through it.

VI. Review—Our children get a Christ-centered makeover when:

A. God is the foundation of our families.

B. We understand God provides and protects.

C. We realize they are a blessing to us and a legacy from us.

D. Families stand strong in the face of life's challenges.

Faith Begins at Home
Sermon Outline #4: The Extended Family Makeover
(Text: 1 & 2 Timothy)

I. Introduction

A. Story—Tell a story about how raising kids to become spiritual champions is hard. Talk about how parents need help. I told a funny story about how before I had kids, I would always joke around with my coworkers when their kids were bad and say, "My kids will never do that!" I then talked about the reality of having kids and how it can be humbling.

B. So how do we transform kids into spiritual champions?

C. Paul was an apostle who took a young man named Timothy under his wing and began to disciple him, began to groom him into a spiritual leader. In the New Testament we have two personal letters Paul writes to Timothy.

1. In these letters we get some insights into this relationship and how Paul, as a spiritual father, was used by God to raise up Timothy as a spiritual champion.

2. Through Paul, Timothy was equipped to pastor and lead through a very difficult church situation in Ephesus.

3. So we are going to hop around this morning through these two letters (and a few other places in Scripture) where Timothy and Paul's relationship is revealed to glean what it takes to raise up kids who are spiritual champions.

D. As we begin, I want to go back to something that we have talked about previously—statistically 3 of the 4 top influences on a person's faith are family members.

1. Mother	81% male	74% female
2. Father	61% male	50% female
3. Pastor	57% male	44% female
4. Grandparent	30% male	29% female

A pastor often takes on the role of an absent father or extended family member.

E. If we open our Bibles to 2 Timothy chapter 1 we will find that Timothy was a lot like many kids in our world today.

 1. 2 Timothy 1:5: "I have been reminded of your sincere faith, which first lived in your grandmother Lois and in your mother Eunice and, I am persuaded, now lives in you also."

 2. Timothy, like many kids today, has a faith that comes from mom and grandma.

 3. Paul comes onto the scene as a guy who fills kind of an extended family role in Timothy's life. Not just as a man outside Timothy's immediate family, but as a pastor filling a absent father, grandparent or extended family role.

F. As we read these personal letters we are going to get a glimpse at how God used Paul to transform Timothy into a spiritual champion and as we do, we are going to receive some insights on how we can become effective extended family members to the kids in our lives and help them to become all that God intends them to be.

II. We become an extended spiritual family when we own the responsibility of mentoring kids spiritually.

A. 2 Timothy 1:2: "To Timothy my dear son"

B. 1 Timothy 1:2: "To Timothy my true son in the faith"

C. Paul didn't tiptoe around his responsibility to raise this kid up as a spiritual champion. He said this is my responsibility.

 1. I'm gonna own it.

 2. I'm gonna claim it.

 3. I'm going to go for it.

D. Do we do that?

 1. Do we unabashedly, accept that we are responsible for the spiritual growth and development of the kids God puts in our lives?

 2. Paul does, he claims it, he owns it—"Timothy my true son in the faith."

　　a. Timothy, let's get it out on the table where everyone, including you and can see that I am taking responsibility for spiritual growth and development in your life.

　　b. And Timothy isn't even his kid.

　　　i. So if you are here this morning and you have tuned me

out because you don't have kids or because your kids are grown and gone or because you don't have grandkids, or because you are single—

    ii. Guess what, Paul was single. He didn't have children or grandchildren of his own, but he still sees it as his responsibility to pass the faith on to the next generation.

E. Maybe you are a grandparent and your grandkids live far away.

    1. First, there are hundreds of kids in this church who could use a spiritual grandparent, dad or friend at (name of your church).

    2. Second, you can still make a difference from a distance.

        a. Story: Tell a story of a grandparent who actively stays connected with their grandkids and intentionally invests in them spiritually.

        b. There is a woman in our church who has a granddaughter who lives literally across the country, but she wants so much for her to know God through a relationship with Jesus Christ that she makes tapes, little cassette tapes, where she records herself singing Bible and worship songs, reading Bible verses and stories and praying for her granddaughter. She could make all the excuses in the world, but distance hasn't prevented her from claiming the responsibility that God wants to use her to transform her granddaughter into a spiritual champion (even from thousands of miles away).

F. Paul owned it friends, he claimed it, he said this is my responsibility. This woman owns it! Do you own the responsibility in the lives of the kids God has put in your life?

III. We become an extended spiritual family when we make prayer and Scripture foundational in our relationships.

A. First of all, Paul let Timothy know he was praying for him.

    1. 2 Timothy 1:3: "I thank God, whom I serve, as my forefathers did, with a clear conscience, as night and day I constantly remember you in my prayers."

    2. Do you pray for your kids?

    3. And perhaps more importantly, do your kids know (and I mean KNOW) that you pray for them?

      a. Do we understand the power and influence that KNOWING someone is praying for you, has on a person?

      b. Story—Share a story of someone who grew up knowing that their grandparent or aunt or adult friend constantly prayed for them. Share how that influenced and impacted that person.

B. Second, Paul also prayed with Timothy!

  1. Six New Testament letters are attributed to both Paul and Timothy. They are the "we."

      a. Colossians 1:3: "We always thank God, the Father of our Lord Jesus Christ, when we pray for you."

      b. Colossians 1:9: "For this reason, since the day we heard about you, we have not stopped praying for you and asking God to fill you with the knowledge of his will through all spiritual wisdom and understanding."

      c. 1 Thessalonians 1:2: "We always thank God for all of you, mentioning you in our prayers."

      d. 1 Thessalonians 5:16-18: "Be joyful always; pray continually; give thanks in all circumstances, for this is God's will for you in Christ Jesus."

      e. 2 Thessalonians 1:11: "We constantly pray for you, that our God may count you worthy of his calling, and that by his power he may fulfill every good purpose of yours and every act prompted by your faith."

  2. Prayer was foundational in Paul's relationship with Timothy.

      a. It was more than just something they did,

      b. More than a routine,

      c. Prayer was woven into the fabric of their relationship.

C. Third, Scripture held a foundational place in the relationship between Paul and Timothy.

  1. In 2 Timothy 3:15-17 Paul says this to Timothy: "From infancy you have known the holy Scriptures, which are able to make you wise for salvation through faith in Christ Jesus. All Scripture is God-breathed and is useful for teaching, rebuking, correcting and training in righteousness, so that the man of God may be thoroughly equipped for every good work."

2. George Barna: "The basis of spiritual training is the Bible. Parents are instructed to rely upon it for truth, values, principles and direction as they nurture their children." (George Barna, *Transforming Children into Spiritual Champions*, Ventura, CA: Regal Books, 2003, p. 83.)

3. Think about the relationships you have with the kids God has placed in your life. If prayer and scripture were taken out of those relationships, how different would they really be?

D. In the relationships with kids where you are being called to raise up spiritual champions are these three elements foundational?

IV. We become an extended spiritual family when we are authentic, vulnerable and humble.

A. 1 Timothy 1:12-16: "[12]I thank Christ Jesus our Lord, who has given me strength, that he considered me faithful, appointing me to his service. [13]Even though I was once a blasphemer and a persecutor and a violent man, I was shown mercy because I acted in ignorance and unbelief. [14]The grace of our Lord was poured out on me abundantly, along with the faith and love that are in Christ Jesus. [15]Here is a trustworthy saying that deserves full acceptance: Christ Jesus came into the world to save sinners—of whom I am the worst. [16]But for that very reason I was shown mercy so that in me, the worst of sinners, Christ Jesus might display his unlimited patience as an example for those who would believe on him and receive eternal life."

B. Now, that kind of a statement may be easy for us to make in general as we recognize that we are sinners, but remember this is a personal letter between a spiritual leader and his disciple.

1. For Paul to be able to say "I am the worst of all sinners" to his spiritual son, the young man who he is trying to raise up to be a spiritual champion, that takes some real authentic humility.

2. That's taking the relationship:

a. From "I'm the leader; you're the follower" and "I'm the teacher; you're the learner"

b. To "I'm learning just like you are and I need the grace of God just like you." And I think that was powerful to Timothy.

C. Example: Share a personally story of a spiritual leader who was authentic and vulnerable with you and how that impacted and encouraged you.

D. George Barna: "Another teaching tool that helps many parents is their willingness to tell personal stories and integrate some degree of personal vulnerability into their narrative in order to capture attention and drive home a point . . . When parents effectively describe a compelling life event that resulted in personal transformation, children are more likely to glean valuable wisdom from the story." (George Barna, *Transforming Children into Spiritual Champions*, Ventura, CA: Regal Books, 2003, p. 86.)

E. Do kids see you as humble, learning, growing, Christians who need God's Grace just as much as they do?

V. We become an extended spiritual family when we encourage and prepare kids to use their gifts.

A. 1 Timothy 4:12-14: "[12]Don't let anyone look down on you because you are young, but set an example for the believers in speech, in life, in love, in faith and in purity. [13]Until I come, devote yourself to the public reading of Scripture, to preaching and to teaching. [14]Do not neglect your gift, which was given you through a prophetic message when the body of elders laid their hands on you."

B. 2 Timothy 1:6-7: "[6]For this reason I remind you to fan into flame the gift of God, which is in you through the laying on of my hands. [7]For God did not give us a spirit of timidity, but a spirit of power, of love and of self-discipline."

C. In other words:

1. Timothy, you've got gifts, use them.

2. Timothy, you are a young man but you are not the church of tomorrow. You are the church of right now and God wants to use you.

D. The situation in Ephesus, where Paul had sent Timothy to serve as pastor or overseer was a tough situation.

1. It was a highly mystical city full of cults, prostitution and heretical teaching about God.

2. But Paul was always preparing Timothy for what he would face and then encouraging him to use his gifts in the face of those challenges. Do we do that with our kids?

E. Story—Share a story of an adult who has empowered and encouraged a kid to use his/her gifts.

F. 2 Timothy 4:2-5: "[2]Preach the Word; be prepared in season and out of season; correct, rebuke and encourage—with great patience and careful instruction. [3]For the time will come when men will not put up with sound doctrine. Instead, to suit their own desires, they will gather around them a great number of teachers to say what their itching ears want to hear. [4]They will turn their ears away from the truth and turn aside to myths. [5]But you, keep your head in all situations, endure hardship, do the work of an evangelist, discharge all the duties of your ministry."

G. Paul was constantly preparing and encouraging Timothy to use his gifts in a world hostile to the truth.

VI. We become an extended spiritual family when we model the Christian life.

A. 2 Timothy 3:10-14: "[10]You, however, know all about my teaching, my way of life, my purpose, faith, patience, love, endurance, [11]persecutions, sufferings—what kinds of things happened to me in Antioch, Iconium and Lystra, the persecutions I endured . . . [14]But as for you, continue in what you have learned and have become convinced of, because you know those from whom you learned it."

B. What Paul is saying here is: Timothy you have spent considerable time with me. You know what living for Christ looks like because you have seen it firsthand in my life!

C. Story: Talk about someone you have watched live the Christian life firsthand and how that impacted you.

D. George Barna: "Our research suggests that behavioral modeling is the most powerful component in a parent's efforts to influence a child. It appears that as our society becomes increasingly secular, our children are developing a hypocrisy detector—an internal sensitivity to actions, attitudes, values and beliefs that are inherently contradictory to words that have been uttered as instructions. When an inconsistency is identified, a child is prone to do two things: (1) ignore the instruction itself; and (2) conclude that there is no specific command that they must obey. . . . If you are struggling with particular aspects of raising your child, especially in relation to the faith dimension, step back and evaluate your behavior. You may discover that while you are able to voice the appropriate concepts to your young ones, your behavior negates those words. The 'do as I say, not as I do' approach is increasingly incompatible with effective influence upon children." (George Barna, *Transforming Children into Spiritual Champions*, Ventura, CA: Regal Books, 2003, p. 85.)

E. Story—I told the story of a man in our church who, after faithfully deciding to get baptized, watched all three of his children follow his example.

F. Friends, if you really want to know what kind of a spiritual champion you are raising up? Look in the mirror.

1. Paul writes to the church in Corinth:

    a. 1 Corinthians 4:16-17: "[16]Therefore I urge you to imitate me. [17]For this reason I am sending to you Timothy, my son whom I love, who is faithful in the Lord. He will remind you of my way of life in Christ Jesus, which agrees with what I teach everywhere in every church."

    b. You want see how I live my life for Christ, look at Timothy, his walk with Christ looks a lot like mine.

2. The apple does not fall far from the tree!

VII. Review—We become an extended spiritual family when we:

A. Own the responsibility of mentoring kids spiritually

B. Make prayer and Scripture foundational in our relationships

C. Are authentic, vulnerable and humble

D. Encourage and prepare kids to use their gifts

E. Model the Christian life

Faith Begins at Home
Sermon Outline #5: The Church Makeover
(Text: Psalm 78)

I. Introduction

A. Start with a story illustrating that our kids will end up looking like us. I told a story about how when I was in junior high I saw a picture of my Dad and thought it was me.

B. Legacy—something received from parents and or ancestors that gets transmitted or passed to the next generation.

    1. Perhaps the most significant legacy any of us receive or pass on is our spiritual legacy—the way we related to, responded to and represented Jesus Christ in this world.

    2. All of us

        a. receive a spiritual legacy from the generation before us

        b. pass on a spiritual legacy to the next generation.

C. Two families that were contemporaries of one another in the 1700s:

    1. Edwards family—Mr. Edwards was a Minister, both he and his wife loved the Lord and were fully committed to serving God. This is what came out of their family over the next 3-5 generations:

        a. 14 College Presidents

        b. 100 College Professors

        c. 30 Judges

        d. 100 members of the Clergy including Jonathan Edwards, the famous American preacher who was part of the "Great Awakening" and preached *Sinners in the Hands of an Angry God*

        e. 60 Physicians

        f. 60 Authors

        g. 100 Lawyers (Well, I guess no family can be perfect.)

    2. Jukes family—At the same time Mr. Edwards lived, there was another

man by the name of Mr. Jukes. Mr. Jukes was a common thief and the legacy he fostered over the next several generations was this:

    a. 300 professional paupers (professional beggars)

    b. 60 thieves

    c. 130 convicted criminals

    d. 55 acts of sexual obsession

    e. Only 20 who ever learned a trade

    f. 10 who served prison time

    g. 7 murderers

    3. Biblical principle illustrated here is: What you do in your life will create a pattern and cycle of behavior that gets passed on to the following generations.

D. Deuteronomy 5:9-10—From the Ten Commandments (significant portion of Scripture): "I, the LORD your God, am a jealous God, punishing the children for the sin of the fathers to the third and fourth generation of those who hate me, but showing love to a thousand generations of those who love me and keep my commandments."

    1. Intentionally used here to make the point of a very serious spiritual reality that is:

        a. What you do, how you live, the faith in and relationship with Jesus Christ that you have does not simply impact you, but it's carried over into the lives of those you love.

        b. "As parents, we pass on things to our children every day. They're watching us, learning from us and emulating us. The question is not *are* we passing things on to our children, but *what* are we passing on to our children."

E. So our church makeover must be to provide real family support! How can we empower families to pass on a saving, transforming, life-changing relationship with Jesus to our kids and the next generation?

F. Psalm 78:1-7

> *1 O my people, hear my teaching;*
>   *listen to the words of my mouth.*

> *2 I will open my mouth in parables,*
>   *I will utter hidden things, things from of old—*

> ³ *what we have heard and known,*
> *what our fathers have told us.*
>
> ⁴ *We will not hide them from their children;*
> *we will tell the next generation*
> *the praiseworthy deeds of the LORD,*
> *his power, and the wonders he has done.*
>
> ⁵ *He decreed statutes for Jacob*
> *and established the law in Israel,*
> *which he commanded our forefathers*
> *to teach their children,*
>
> ⁶ *so the next generation would know them,*
> *even the children yet to be born,*
> *and they in turn would tell their children.*
>
> ⁷ *Then they would put their trust in God*
> *and would not forget his deeds*
> *but would keep his commands.*

II. As a church we must empower families to continuously talk about God.

A. Psalm 78:3-4

> ³ *what we have heard and known,*
> *what our fathers have told us.*
>
> ⁴ *We will not hide them from their children;*
> *we will tell the next generation*
> *the praiseworthy deeds of the LORD,*
> *his power, and the wonders he has done.*

B. John Piper: "If there is one memory that our children should have of our families and of our church it is this; they should remember God. God was first. God was central. There was a passion for the supremacy of God in all things" (www.desiringGod.org [accessed November 2007]).

C. When we talk about God with our children, we must talk about both

1. what we've heard and

2. what we've known.

D. In church we are really good at talking with our kids about:

1. What we've heard.

   a. What we've been told or

   b. What we've read about in the Bible.

   c. The experiences of other people

      i.   Jonah's experience with the whale

      ii. Moses's experience with the 10 Plagues

      iii. Noah's experience of building the ark, and the flood

      iv. The disciples' experiences of watching Jesus

         (A) Walk on water

         (B) Healing the blind and lame

         (C) Calm the storm

         (D) Feed the 5,000 and

         (E) Raise Lazarus from the dead

2. But friends, I'm convinced that what our kids need and long for is to hear

   a. OUR Testimonies,

   b. OUR Experiences and

   c. OUR Personal encounters with the living God

      i.   "Hey Johnny, you know what God did in Daddy's life today at work?"

      ii. "Hey Emma, remember how you and Gramma have been praying for your friend to get better?"

      iii. "Hey Sammy (use your child's name), have I ever told you the story of when your Daddy gave his life to Jesus?"

E. A spiritual legacy begins with our kids knowing and understanding that they belong to a church, to a family, where people always have and still do experience the "praiseworthy deeds of the LORD, his power, and the wonders he has done" (v. 4).

F. Share examples of how the church does or could empower parents to talk with their kids about God. (I talked about the take-home paper our kids bring home from Sunday School each week. I also talked about an upcoming Take It Home Event on family devotions.)

G. "If we want our children to have a faith that influences the way they live their lives, then in our homes we need to be modeling faith through a personal relationship with Jesus Christ."

III. As a church, we must empower families to teach children to live by the Word of God.

A. Psalm 78:5: "He decreed statutes for Jacob and established the law in Israel, which he commanded our forefathers to teach their children."

B. "The Bible has helped families for generations gone by and it will continue to help families for generations to come. Will you let it help you?"

C. Satan is waging all out war, using every resource he can to steal the minds and hearts of our kids.

1. TV

2. Internet

3. Music

4. Video games

5. Magazines

D. "As you bring Christ into the center of your home, you'll always have a way out of any situation Satan throws at your family."

E. We have got to be intentional and proactive in teaching our kids

1. The statues

2. The decrees

3. What following God in this world (where they live) looks like

F. Share about ways your church is or could partner with parents to help kids live by the Law of God. (I shared about our upcoming Dating Kissing, Sex & Stuff retreat.)

G. God has given us His Word, we must be intentional and proactive in teaching it and applying it.

IV. As a church, we must empower families to develop real understanding of God's law.

A. Psalm 78:6: "so the next generation would know them, even the children yet to be born, and they in turn would tell their children."

B. "know"—understand; experience; care for; an intimate relationship with; able to teach

C. Tell a story illustrating the power of really understanding something and not just knowing the correct answers. I talked about how my brother is an engineering professor and that he understands the mathematics enough to explain them to his students.

D. 1 Peter 3:15: "But in your hearts set apart Christ as Lord. Always be prepared to give an answer to everyone who asks you to give the reason for the hope that you have. But do this with gentleness and respect." Our kids must understand and own the gospel to the point that they can respond when the need to.

V. As a church, we must empower families to see obedience as the result of trusting God.

A. Psalm 78:7: "Then they would put their trust in God and would not forget his deeds but would keep his commands."

B. This final verse is about trust and obedience. About future generations following God in their

1. Decisions

2. Actions

3. Choices and

4. Behaviors

C. Interestingly enough, the trust comes first. This passage does not say, "If you make your kids obey, then they will come to know Jesus." It doesn't say, "Here is a list of rules for your kids to follow, if you enforce these, they'll grow up to have a personal saving relationship with Me."

D. Sometimes I think we interpret "Train a child in the way he should go, and when he is old he will not turn from it" (Proverbs 22:6) to mean:

1. No Cussing

2. No Smoking

3. No Dating till You're 27

4. No Drinking

5. No Drugs and

6. No rated R Movies

(Some good rules in there by the way!)

E. However:

1. If the foundation of these rules is not relationship

2. Then rules will lead to rebellion!

F. All of us who have kids want them to make God-honoring decisions and in the short term we sometimes have to direct those decisions with rules. However, in the long-term, true obedience will only come through a knowledge and trust of the living God.

VI. Closing

A. As a church, we need a makeover.

B. We need to focus on providing real support to families, empowering them to pass on a

1. Saving

2. Transforming

3. Life-changing relationship with Jesus

To the next generation.

C. We can't do if for you, but we'll do it with you.

D. We can't take that responsibility from you, but we are committed to walking along side you.

F. If you involve yourself, if you engage, we will do everything we can to give you real family support!